QuickClicks

D0211519

MICROSOFT®

EXCEL® 2010

CAREERTRACK®

QuickClicks Microsoft Excel 2010 Reference Guide

Trademarks

Disclaimer

The QuickClicks Reference Guide series is dedicated to all of CareerTrack's devoted customers. Our customers' commitment to continuing education and professional development inspired the creation of the award-winning *Unlocking the Secrets* CD-ROM series and the *QuickClicks Reference Guide* series.

Thank you for your continued support!

Contents

Introduction

Congratulations on your purchase of QuickClicks: Microsoft Excel 2010. You have invested wisely in yourself and taken a step forward in your personal and professional development. This reference guide is an important tool in your productivity toolbox. By effectively using the tools and functions within Microsoft Excel, you will be able to maximize your efficiency. The tips in this reference guide are written for the user who has a basic understanding of data processing and at least one year of experience using other Microsoft Office applications.

Anatomy of a Tip

Each tip displays the tip title in the top left corner and the tip category in the top right, so you always know where you are and what you are learning. Each tip is written in plain English. Some tips will include a "What Microsoft Calls It" reference to help you perform more effective searches for additional feature capabilities in Microsoft's help system.

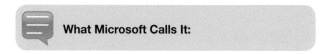

What Microsoft Calls It:

Each tip is assigned a difficulty value from one to four, with one circle representing the easiest tips and four circles representing the hardest.

Difficulty: ●○○○

All tips begin with a business scenario, identified as **PROBLEM**.

SOLUTION explains how the demonstrated feature might be used to solve the problem. A set of easy-to-understand instructions follows.

Extras Include the Following

Icon	Name	What It Means
	Bright Idea	Bright ideas provide additional information about Excel or the features in question.
	Hot Tip	Hot Tips share related functions and features, or additional features and uses of the task being demonstrated.
	Caution	Cautions draw attention to situations where you might find yourself tripped up by a particularly complicated operation, instances when making an incorrect choice will cause errors you will have to correct, or times when very similar options might be confusing.

There are two other bonuses that do not have miniature icons. They are displayed at the end of tips, where appropriate. These are:

Icon	Name	What It Means
	Options	Options represent places where there are two or more ways to accomplish a task or where two or more results might be obtained, depending on the choices you make. Option icons appear within the text, and all relevant choices are next to the icon.
	Quickest Click	Quickest Clicks indicate there is a faster way to accomplish the same task taught in the tip. Shortcuts like this, though, may leave out important steps that help you understand the feature. Therefore, each tip teaches the most complete method for accomplishing a task, and a Microsoft Quickest Click appears if there is a faster option.

At the bottom of each page, you will see either a Continue or a Stop icon. These icons indicate whether a tip continues on the next page or if it is complete.

Find Your Way Around

Items You'll See in the Excel Window

The tips are written in plain English, but there is no way to get completely away from using some technical terms. What follows are three maps that show you what this book calls various features in Microsoft Excel.

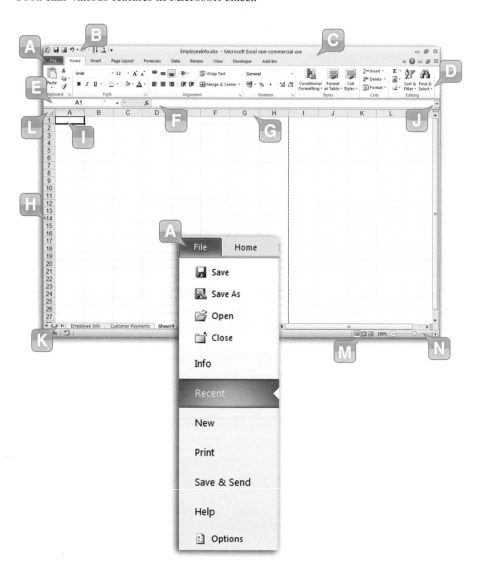

The Excel Window

A File Tab	Click this tab to see the Office Backstage view. Find open, save, and print options. Manage files and access Excel Options menus.
B Quick Access Toolbar	Place items here for quick and easy access.
C Title Bar	View the title and file type of the active document.
D Ribbon	Locate Excel menu items and controls.
E Name Box	Give a cell a name.
F Formula Bar	Enter data or type a formula or function.
G Column Headers	Click to select an entire column or use the letter in formulas and functions.
H Row Headers	Click to select an entire row or use the number in formulas and functions.
I Active Cell	The black border indicates the currently active cell or range.
J Formula Bar Expander	Expand the formula bar to view long formulas and functions.
K Sheet Tabs and Navigation Controls	These allow you to select sheets, move between sheets, and add/delete sheets.
L Select Sheet Button	Click to select the entire active sheet.
M Workbook View Shortcut Buttons	Click to toggle between normal, page layout, and page break preview view.
N Zoom Slider	Slide to zoom workbook magnification in or out.

Items You'll See on the Ribbon

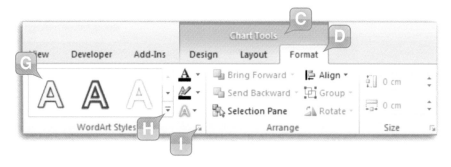

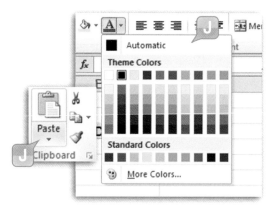

Items You'll See on the Ribbon

A Tab	Collections of related features and functions.	
B Group	Collections of related controls.	
C Highlighted Ribbon Section	Contextual ribbon sections appear when some items are selected or used.	
D Contextual Tabs	Some specialized tabs only appear when a particular feature is active. These special tabs usually appear in conjunction with a highlighted ribbon section.	
E Buttons	Buttons are single-click controls that perform one function.	
F Dropdown Menus and Dropdown Buttons	Some buttons have a graphic and a down-pointing arrow, while others have a default selection visible, followed by a down arrow. Clicking the arrow reveals additional choices.	
G Selection Box	A panel containing a list of selectable items.	
H Panel Launcher	A scroll control that can be clicked to launch a selection panel.	
I Dialog Box Launcher	A special group control that launches a related dialog box.	
J Combo Button	These controls are split into two parts to function as both a button and a dropdown. They may be split horizontally or vertically.	

Items You'll See in Menus and Dialog Boxes

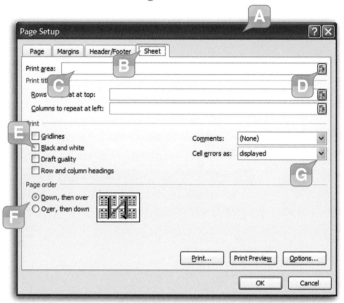

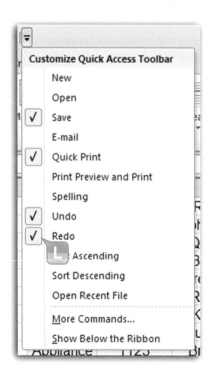

Items You'll See in Menus and Dialog Boxes

A	Dialog Box	A feature-specific box that you can launch to control various functions in Excel.
B	Tabs	Some dialog boxes have tabs similar to the ones on the ribbon. Each tab is focused on a particular subset of features.
C	Textbox	A box where text can be typed.
D	Selection Tool	A button that, when pressed, minimizes the dialog box that houses it and allows direct selection of cells.
E	Checkbox	A box that activates the related selection when checked and deactivates it when unchecked. More than one checkbox may be checked in a series.
F	Radio Button	A circle that activates the related selection when selected and deactivates it when deselected. Only one radio button may be selected in a series.
G	Dropdown Menu	A simple down-pointing arrow button that reveals a set of selectable choices.
H	Right-Click Menu	This two-part menu appears when you right-click anywhere on the sheet.
I	Dialog Box Launcher	In menus, selections that launch dialog boxes are followed by ellipses (…).
J	Menu Launcher	Menu selections that open additional menus are followed by right-pointing arrows.
K	Shortcut Keys	Menu selections that can be launched by a keystroke on your keyboard are identified by the underlined letters in them. Click any underlined letter in a menu to launch that selection's function.
L	Toggle Checkmarks	Some menus have checkmarks. Clicking an unchecked item in those lists checks it and activates the selected option. Clicking a checked item unchecks it and deactivates the selected option.

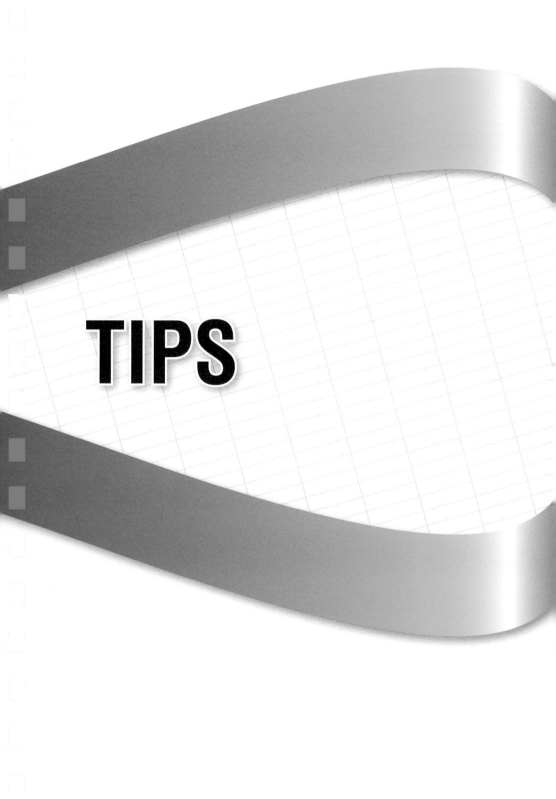

TIPS

1 | Customize Your Excel Environment

Difficulty: ⬤○○○

PROBLEM There are several actions and commands you use frequently, but they are spread across multiple tabs and are often several clicks deep. It would be helpful if they were more accessible to match your personal work style or the needs of your business.

SOLUTION Because Excel is designed to enhance productivity, Microsoft has provided ways for organizations and users to customize their workspaces and experience.

Some customization is achieved by adding options to the **Quick Access Toolbar** or the **Action Bar**, but the most robust changes are accessible from the **Excel Options** screen.

What Microsoft Calls It: Customize User Preferences

See Also: Customize the Quick Access Toolbar; Customize the Ribbon

Step-by-Step

Set User Preferences in Excel

1. Click the **File** tab **A**.

2. Click the **Excel Options** button **B** to launch the **Excel Options** dialog box.

3. Make adjustments within the menu options **C**.

   - **General:** Change some basic defaults within Excel, including interface options and new workbook settings, and personalize your copy of Excel.

   - **Formulas:** Adjust options related to formula calculation, performance and error checking.

   - **Proofing:** Modify how Excel corrects and formats text.

- **Save:** Decide how and how often workbooks are saved.

- **Language:** Choose your Office language preferences for proofing (spelling, grammar, etc.) and Help texts.

- **Advanced:** Modify additional Excel settings. Note that many of the settings adjusted here have ramifications that should be carefully considered before changes are made.

- **Customize Ribbon:** Add/remove or regroup items on the Ribbon.

- **Quick Access Toolbar:** Add/remove items to/from the **Quick Access Toolbar.**

- **Add-Ins:** Manage your Excel **Add-Ins**. Note that most installed **Add-Ins** will not appear on the **Add-Ins tab** unless they are active.

- **Trust Center:** Manage workbook security settings.

4. Click the **OK** button.

2 | Manage Your Files in the Backstage View

Difficulty: ⬤◯◯◯

PROBLEM You manage several workbooks every week. Not only do you create new workbooks on a regular basis, but you also update, edit, and share many existing files. You need to know how to keep all these files organized and where to find file management tools that will help you work more efficiently.

SOLUTION Take advantage of the features available in Excel 2010's **Backstage**.

In Excel 2010, the **Office** button is replaced by the **File** tab. Clicking the **File** tab takes you to the place in Excel where you will manage your files and the data about them—creating, saving, security options, and customized settings. It is where you will find everything you want to do *to* a file that you don't do *in* the file.

Step-by-Step

1. Click the **File** tab **A** to access the view.

    *   The **Info** **B** tab will be selected by default. From the **Info** tab you can manage permissions from the **Protect Workbook** button **C**, compatibility options under the **Check for Issues** button **D**, and version control under the **Manage Versions** button **E**. The **Properties** pane **F** gives you file data such as size, dates modified, and author.

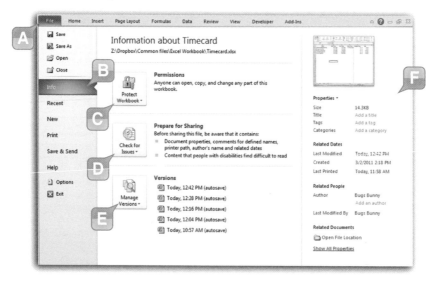

- Your most common tasks such as **Save**, **Save As**, **Open**, and **Close** are located at the top of the **File** menu 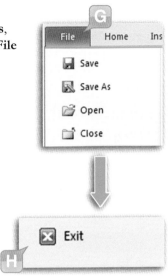. **Exit** is located at the bottom.

- The **Recent** tab opens a pane that displays the most **Recent Workbooks** you have opened. Recently accessed folders and file paths are displayed in the **Recent Places** pane.

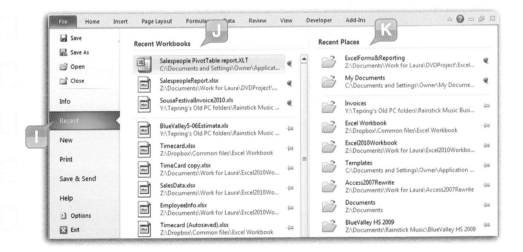

- The **New** tab  is where you will open a new workbook by choosing from Excel's many built-in **Available Templates** . More templates are available under the **Office.com Templates** heading (internet connection required). A preview of each template will appear in the **Preview Pane** . Click the **Create** button to open the template you've chosen.

- The **Print** tab offers some of the most common print options under the **Settings** heading , including Print Area, Pages, Collation, Orientation, Paper size, Margin settings, and Scaling. Check the **Print Preview** pane frequently to see how your data will be displayed as you are working with it.

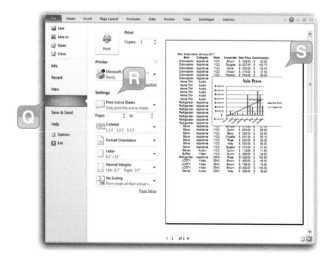

- The **Save & Send** tab is where you will find tools to share your documents via email, the Web, or SharePoint.

- The **Help** tab is where you can go to find answers to questions and problems you may have.

- The **Options** tab launches the **Excel Options** dialog box.

 Hot Tip: Use the **Recent** tab to open files you access frequently without having to browse through many folders to find them.

- If you open many documents every day, you can **Pin** your most important documents to the top of the list. Click any grey pin  on the **Recent Workbooks** or **Recent Places** lists. The pin will turn blue and the file will jump to the top of the list, where it will remain until you unpin it. Click the blue pin to unpin the item.

3 | Adjust Row Height and Column Width

Difficulty: ●○○○

PROBLEM You have created a spreadsheet with the names of your employees, their email addresses, their annual salary, and other employment data. You open the document to refer to during a benefits meeting, but the information you need is not available at a glance.

Long strings or passages of text are truncated **A** or appear to have spilled into the next cell **B**. Numbers appear as "#" signs **C** when there is not enough room to display them in full.

At times you can tell that a row needs more space **D**, but information may stay hidden and you can't tell. In the Benefits column **E** of the illustration, there are multiple rows of text hidden by the inadequate row height.

SOLUTION Adjusting the widths of the columns and the heights of the rows allows you to improve the appearance and usability of your spreadsheet.

There are two methods that can be used to adjust row height and column width:

- **Use the Mouse:** Click and drag to make adjustments using your eyes as a guide for the appropriate size.
- **Use the Format Menu:** Adjust the width in a dialog box.

Step-by-Step

Use the Mouse. Use this option when you need to change a few rows or columns to accommodate longer cell data.

1. Click a numbered row header **F** or lettered column header **G** to select that row/column for adjustment.

2. Move the pointer to the right border of a selected column's header (or the bottom border of a selected row's header) until the pointer changes into a plus sign with up and down or right and left arrowheads (✛) **H**.

3. Click and drag the border right or left (or up or down) to the width (or height) you desire. As you drag, the new border is identified by a dotted line **I** and the current measurement displays in a message box **J**.

4. Release the mouse when you are at the desired width **K**.

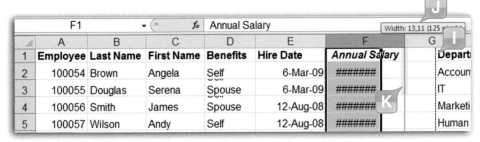

3 Adjust Row Height and Column Width
(continued)

Step-by-Step

Use the Format Menu. Use this option when you need to adjust row height (or column width) for many rows or an entire sheet.

1. Select the rows you want to adjust.

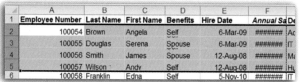

2. On the **Home** tab, click the **Format** button **K** in the **Cells** group.

3. Select **Row Height** **L**. The **Row Height** dialog appears. *Note: This dialog can also be accessed by right-clicking on a cell.*

4. Enter a new height value in points (there are 72 points to an inch) in the **Row Height** textbox **M**.

5. Click the **OK** button **N**.

6. This adjusts all rows to the same height, regardless of the amount of information in each cell.

Bright Idea: To select more than one adjacent row or column, click and drag to make your selections. To select more than one non-adjacent row or column, hold the CTRL key while you click row headers to select your rows.

 Hot Tip: Select an entire sheet by clicking the Select Sheet button (▨) Ⓞ or by pressing **CTRL+A** on your keyboard.

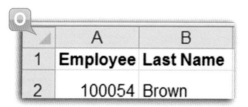

	A	B
1	**Employee**	**Last Name**
2	100054	Brown

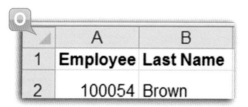 **Quickest Click:** Fit row height or column width to match the contents of the cells in an entire selection at once. To do so, first select the cells to adjust. Next, move the pointer to the space between any two row or column headers until you see it change to a plus sign with arrows (╬), then double-click. The rows/columns automatically adjust to fit the content.

	A	B	C	D	E	F
1	**Employee Number**	**Last Name**	**First Name**	**Benefits**	**Hire Date**	**Annual Salary**
2	100054	Brown	Angela	Self	6-Mar-09	$ 47 000,00
3	100055	Douglas	Serena	Self Spouse	6-Mar-09	$ 52 000,00
4	100056	Smith	James	Self Spouse Children	12-Aug-08	$ 35 000,00
5	100057	Wilson	Andy	Self	12-Aug-08	$ 67 000,00
6	100058	Franklin	Edna	Self	5-Nov-10	$ 52 000,00

STOP

4 | Hide and Unhide Columns and Rows

Difficulty: ●○○○

PROBLEM You have created a worksheet that you plan to share at a meeting. Parts of the information included in the sheet are confidential and other columns contain data that is irrelevant to the others who will use it. You don't want to lose the data, but you also don't want to make a new worksheet from scratch.

SOLUTION The **Hide/Unhide** feature allows you to keep the data but make it invisible. In the example below, the Annual Salary column has been hidden from view. 🔥

	A	B	C	D	E	G
1	Employee Number	Last Name	First Name	Benefits	Hire Date	Department
2	100054	Brown	Angela	Self	6-Mar-09	Accounting
3	100055	Douglas	Serena	Spouse	6-Mar-09	IT
4	100056	Smith	James	Spouse	12-Aug-08	Marketing
5	100057	Wilson	Andy	Self	12-Aug-08	Human Resources
6	100058	Franklin	Edna	Self	5-Nov-10	IT
7	100059	Rory	Hawkins	-	6-Mar-03	Sales
8	100060	Johnson	Kim	Self	5-Nov-10	Accounting

	A	B	C	D	E	F	G
1	Employee Number	Last Name	First Name	Benefits	Hire Date	Annual Salary	Department
2	100054	Brown	Angela	Self	6-Mar-09	$ 47,000.00	Accounting
3	100055	Douglas	Serena	Spouse	6-Mar-09	$ 52,000.00	IT
4	100056	Smith	James	Spouse	12-Aug-08	$ 35,000.00	Marketing
5	100057	Wilson	Andy	Self	12-Aug-08	$ 67,000.00	Human Resources
6	100058	Franklin	Edna	Self	5-Nov-10	$ 52,000.00	IT
7	100059	Rory	Hawkins	-	6-Mar-03	$ 33,000.00	Sales
8	100060	Johnson	Kim	Self	5-Nov-10	$ 45,000.00	Accounting

🪜 Step-by-Step

Hide/Unhide Columns or Rows

1. Click the lettered column header or numbered row header of the columns or rows to be hidden . *Note: When unhiding, you need to select the columns/rows adjacent to the hidden one.* 💡

	A	B	C	D	E	F	G
1	Employee Number	Last Name	First Name	Benefits	Hire Date	Annual Salary	Department
2	100054	Brown	Angela	Self	6-Mar-09	$ 47,000.00	Accounting
3	100055	Douglas	Serena	Spouse	6-Mar-09	$ 52,000.00	IT
4	100056	Smith	James	Spouse	12-Aug-08	$ 35,000.00	Marketing

2. Click on the **Home** tab.

3. In the **Cells** panel, click the **Format** button and then select **Hide & Unhide** and your selection .

   • **Hide Rows:** Hides the selected row(s).
   • **Hide Columns:** Hides the selected column(s).
   • **Hide Sheet:** Hides the whole active worksheet.
   • **Unhide Rows:** Unhides any hidden rows within the selected area.
   • **Unhide Columns:** Unhides any hidden columns within the selected area.

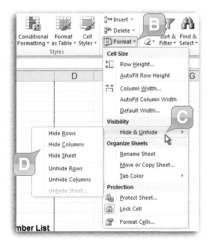

Hot Tip: Hide an entire worksheet by right-clicking its tab and selecting **Hide** from the fly-out menu that appears.

Bright Idea: To select more than one adjacent row or column, click and drag to make your selections. To select more than one non-adjacent row or column, hold the **CTRL** key while you click row headers to select your rows.

Quickest Click: Select the columns or rows you want to hide. Right-click your selection and choose **Hide** or **Unhide** from the right-click menu .

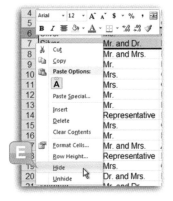

5 | Freeze and Unfreeze Columns and Rows

Difficulty: ●○○○

PROBLEM You are working with an extremely large worksheet and find that when you scroll down or over to the data you want to review, you can't recall which column or row contains the data you need.

SOLUTION Freeze columns and rows so they are always visible, even when you scroll. Freezing columns keeps them visible while you scroll to the right. Freezing rows keeps them visible while you scroll down. By freezing the first column **A**, you will keep headers, like Employee Number, in place as you look for data in the far right columns.

Likewise, by freezing the first row **B**, you keep row headers, like employee data categories, in place as you scroll down in your spreadsheet. ⚠

	A	B	C	D	E
1	Employee Number	Last Name	First Name	Benefits	Hire Date
2	100054	Brown	Angela	Self	6-Mar-09
3	100055	Douglas	Serena	Self Spouse	6-Mar-09
4	100056	Smith	James	Self Spouse Children	12-Aug-08

	A	B	C	D	E
1	Employee Number	Last Name	First Name	Benefits	Hire Date
8	100060	Johnson	Kim	Self	5-Nov-10
9	100070	Quinn	Aidan	Self Children	6-Mar-09
10	100075	Berry	Andy	Self Spouse	5-Nov-10
11	100087	Crocker	Becky	Self	12-Aug-08

	A	E	F	G
1	Employee Number	Hire Date	Annual Salary	Department
2	100054	6-Mar-09	$ 47,000.00	Accounting
3	100055	6-Mar-09	$ 52,000.00	IT
4	100056	12-Aug-08	$ 35,000.00	Marketing

Step-by-Step

Freeze a Column or a Row

1. Place your cursor in the cell to the right and/or below where you want the freezing lines to be drawn.

    - Click cell A2 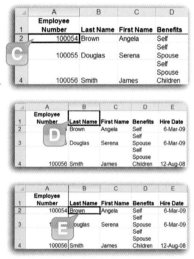 to freeze the top row.
    - Click cell B1 to freeze the first column.
    - Click cell B2 to freeze the top row and the left column.
    - Click cell A1 to freeze your sheet along vertical and horizontal midpoints.
    - Click in any other cell to freeze all rows above and columns to the left of the selection.

2. On the **View** tab in the **Window** group, click the **Freeze Panes** dropdown and select **Freeze Panes** .

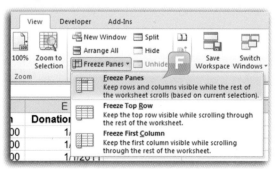

Unfreezing Columns and Rows

On the **View** tab in the **Window** group, click the **Freeze Panes** dropdown and select **Unfreeze Panes** 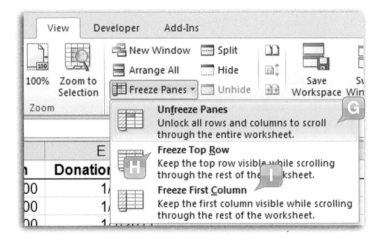.

Caution: At first it can be tricky to figure out which cell to click to freeze the right rows and columns. Try freezing and unfreezing a few times until you get the hang of it.

Quickest Click: Freeze the Top Row or First Column
You can quickly freeze the top row or left column by selecting the **Freeze Top Row** [H] or **Freeze First Column** [I] options from the **Freeze Panes** dropdown in the **Window** group of the **View** tab.

6 | Choose a File Format When Saving a Workbook

Difficulty: ●○○○

PROBLEM The document you have just finished will need to be reviewed by collaborators who have different versions of Excel. When the document is approved, the data will need to be prepared for export and inclusion on a Web page. You want to save a document (or a copy of a document) that others can use and will meet your specific requirements.

SOLUTION Use the **Save As** command rather than simply hitting the **Save** button on the **Quick Access Toolbar** (or in the **File** menu). Microsoft offers you many options when it comes to file types and formats, each with its own purposes. Collaborating with people who have different versions of Excel, security concerns, tracking changes, preparing data for export, or readying your worksheet for inclusion on a web page are all reasons you may decide against a default 2007 .XLXS file.

Step-by-Step

Choose a File Format When Saving a Workbook

1. Click on the **File** tab **A**.

2. Click **Save As** **B**. The **Save As** dialog box **C** will open.

3. Type in a file name for your workbook in the **File name:** text box **D**.

4. Select a file type from the **Save as type:** dropdown menu **E**.

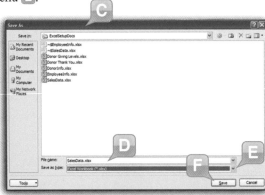

- **Excel Workbook (.XLSX):** This is the default 2010 file format.

- **Excel Macro-Enabled Workbook (.XLSM):** This format is essentially the same as the default format, except that it can store VBA code. If you include VBA code, you will be prompted to save in this format. .XLTM is the template version of this format.

- **Excel Binary Workbook (.XLSB):** This is the fastest-loading file format and accommodates VBA. It is not, however, an XML format and is not ideal for data management without Excel 2007 or 2010. There are also security concerns associated with this format.

- **Excel 97-2003 Workbook (.XLS):** This is a format fully accessible by previous versions of Excel back to 97. The .XLT format, 97-2003 template, is also available.

- **PDF and XPS:** .PDF and .XPS are read-only formats that will produce documents that are easy to read, share, and print.

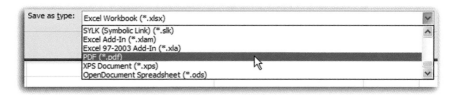

- **Other Formats:** Other formats are available, such as .HTML (for the web), .TXT (text only), and .CSV (Comma Separated Value).

5. Click the **Save** button .

7 | Merge and Unmerge Cells

Difficulty: ●○○○

PROBLEM You are working with a sheet that contains several different types of information and you want to clarify the data by using labels. You have done this by giving groups of columns the same heading, but it looks cluttered and repetitive.

SOLUTION Merge the cells that have the same heading into one large cell that spans all the relevant columns. Center the heading text for a neat look.

There are several options for merging, all found in the **Merge and Split** menu 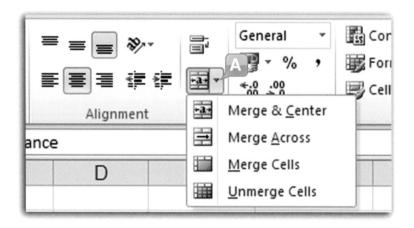 accessed from the **Merge & Center** dropdown button in the **Alignment** group of the **Home** tab.

Merge & Center: Merges selected cells and centers cell contents in the resulting cell.

- **Merge Across:** Merges selected cells into rows along existing row dividers and left-justifies cell contents in the resulting cell(s).

- **Merge Cells:** Merges cells across column and row dividers and left-justifies cell contents in the resulting cell.

- **Unmerge Cells:** Unmerges all merged cells in the selected areas.

  Merging and splitting cells works differently in Excel than it does in other Microsoft Office programs. While helpful, the operations have more rules and consequences and therefore require a bit more planning. ⚠

Step-by-Step

Merge Cells

1. Select the cells you want to merge .
2. On the **Home** tab, click the **Merge & Center** button **C** in the **Alignment** group.
3. Review your merged data **D**.

Split a Merged Cell

1. Select the merged cell you want to split.
2. On the **Home** tab, click the **Merge & Center** button in the **Alignment** group.
3. Click **Unmerge.**

> **Caution:** Merging and splitting are easy but can have some serious consequences.

- After you perform a merge, you will experience difficulties using the lettered headers to select an entire column, or the numbered headers to select an entire row. You can still use the **CTRL** and **SHIFT** keys to select several cells, but you will no longer be able to select large regions around the merge with a single click.

- If you attempt to merge cells that contain data, you may receive an error warning you that some of the cell contents will be lost.

- When unmerging merged cells, you need to perform one split at a time to avoid data loss.

8 Create Your Own Styles or Format

Difficulty: ◯◯◯◯

PROBLEM Your department regularly works with a set of similar but inconsistent worksheets. Some documents may display the same data in different formats—such as the date; for example, "11/24/74" is equivalent to "November 24, 1974"—while others use similar colors on different columns and rows. The information is difficult to find and read when every sheet is different. Errors are then introduced when people enter data in the wrong format or wrong place.

SOLUTION Create an Excel **Style** for your department's worksheets.

Excel includes many options to control the appearance of numbers, text, and cells. **Styles**, pre-set formats, streamline the formatting process to quickly apply a consistent look across all of your workbooks. Forcing data into a single format means that no matter how people enter the information, it will be reformatted for clarity. Consistency means fewer errors, a unified and professional look, and at-a-glance answers.

View and use a wide range of pre-set styles available in Excel with the **Style Gallery**, accessed via the **Cell Styles** button in the **Styles** group of the Home tab. Even with the wide variety of provided styles, there are times when you want to create your own.

See Also: Copy Styles to Other Workbooks

What Microsoft Calls It: Custom Styles

 Step-by-Step

---

Create a Custom Style

1. Format a cell and its contents the way you would like to save as a **Custom Style**. Settings include: Number, Alignment, Font, Border, Fill, and Protection.

2. Select your formatted cell **A**.

◢	A	B	C	D
1	**Last Name**	**First Name**	**Hire Date**	*Annual Salary*
2	Brown	Angela	6-Mar-09	$ 47,000.00
3	Douglas	Serena	6-Mar-09	$ 52,000.00
4	Smith	James	12-Aug-08	$ 35,000.00

3. Click the **Cell Styles** button **B** in the **Styles** group of the **Home** tab to open the **Style Gallery C**.

4. Click on **New Cell Style** 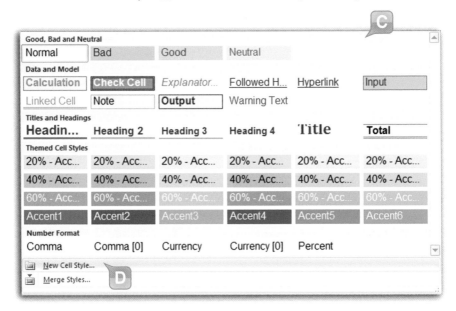 at the bottom of the **Style Gallery.**

5. Type in a name for your **Custom Style** in the **Style name:** textbox ☐ of the **Style** dialog box.

6. Click the **OK** button ☐.

Bright Idea: Use the **Format Painter**, accessed via the **Format Painter** button in the **Clipboard** group of the **Home** tab, to apply styles.

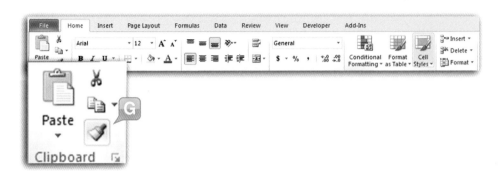

9 Copy Styles to Other Workbooks

Difficulty: ⬤⬤◯◯

PROBLEM You spent a great deal of time customizing a workbook to have exactly the look and feel you want. Your team is familiar with the layout and the data is displayed in at-a-glance efficiency. You want to use this format again without spending even more time re-creating it in a new workbook.

SOLUTION Copy your style. Once you have established styles—whether they are standard Microsoft styles or custom styles you have developed yourself—you can copy them from one workbook to any other. 💡

See Also: Create Your Own Style or Format

🪜 Step-by-Step

1. Open the file containing the **Custom Style** you want to copy to another workbook.

2. Open the workbook to which you wish to copy the selected **Custom Style**.

3. Click the **Cell Styles** button Ⓐ in the **Styles** group of the **Home** tab to open the **Style Gallery** Ⓑ. Select **Merge Styles** Ⓒ at the bottom of the **Style Gallery** to open the **Merge Styles** dialog box Ⓓ.

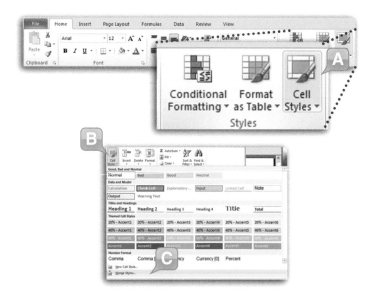

4. Select the workbook that contains the styles you want to copy from the **Merge styles from:** options. ⚠

5. Click the **OK** button ▣.

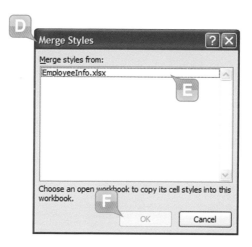

 Hot Tip: You don't have to copy each style individually. When you copy styles from one workbook to another, Excel pulls all saved styles at once.

Caution: Each style in a workbook must have a unique name. A warning appears if you try to copy a style into a workbook that already contains a style with the same name. If you want to replace the existing style with the new one of the same name, click **Yes**. If not, click **No** and rename the styles before attempting the merge again.

10 | Convert Text to Numbers

Difficulty: ●○○○

PROBLEM You have transferred data from an external source into Excel and numbers were mistaken for text. This is causing problems on your worksheet in the form of notation Ⓐ and formula Ⓑ errors.

SOLUTION Convert the text to numbers.

Excel provides two options to accomplish the conversion: Reformat the cells as Number Ⓒ, or multiply each cell by one using the **Paste Special** function. The first option is fastest, but occasionally creates irregularities (often as a result of how the data was entered originally.) The second option, however, produces more consistent results.

See Also: Apply Simple Formatting to Numbers, Dates, and Times; Apply Advanced Formatting to Numbers, Dates, and Times

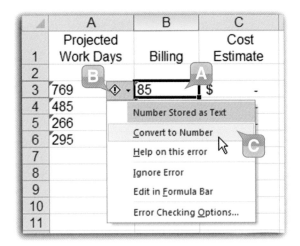

Step-by-Step

Convert Data with the Paste Special Function

Use this method to ensure the data is correctly converted for use in formulas and equations.

1. Enter "1" into any nearby empty cell **D**. Make sure the format of the cell is set to **General** in the **Number** panel on the **Home** tab **E**.

2. Right-click the cell containing the "1" and select **Copy**, or press **CTRL+C** on your keyboard.

3. Select the cells you want to convert **F**.

4. Right-click the selection and choose **Paste Special** **G** to launch the **Paste Special** dialog box **H**.

5. Click on the **Multiply** radio button **I**.

6. Click the **OK** button. **J** ◊

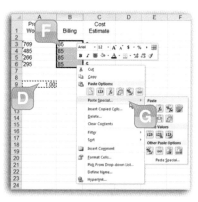

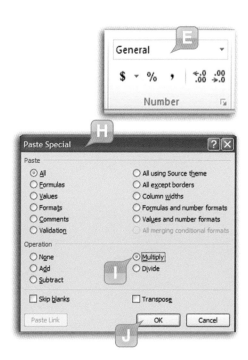

Hot Tip: You may need to re-enter any formulas that were broken because of the columns that were formatted as text. Once you have re-entered them, they should work.

	A	B	C
	Projected Work Days	Billing	Cost Estimate
1			
2			
3	11.00	85.00	$ 935
4	22.00	85.00	$ 1,870
5	10.00	85.00	$ 850
6	33.00	85.00	$ 2,805
7			
8			
9	1.00		

Quickest Click: Select the cells you want to convert, then click the number format dropdown 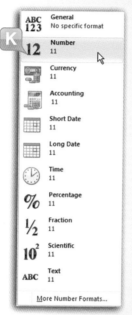 in the **Number** group of the **Home** tab and select **Number** .

You may also choose to right-click the selection and select **Format Cells** , or press **CTRL+1** on the keyboard to open the **Format Cells** dialog box. Once you have the dialog box open, use the options on the **Number** tab to make your adjustments.

11

Apply Simple Formatting to Numbers, Dates, and Times

Difficulty: ●○○○

PROBLEM You have been asked to generate a report to the head of your department along with all the other departments that report to her. To keep the documents consistent, she has asked that you present your data in specific accounting formats.

SOLUTION Apply a number format via the **Number** group controls. Excel provides a multitude of preset formatting options for customizing numbers, dates, and times. Present data in the way that best expresses your needs and conforms with any government, industry or company standards, and styles that might apply to your data.

See Also: Convert Text to Numbers; Apply Advanced Formatting to Numbers, Dates, and Times

---

Step-by-Step

Apply a Simple Number Format via the Number Group Controls

1. Select your cells to be formatted.

2. On the **Home** tab, select a format button from the **Number** panel A, or click the numbers format dropdown B to choose from additional options.

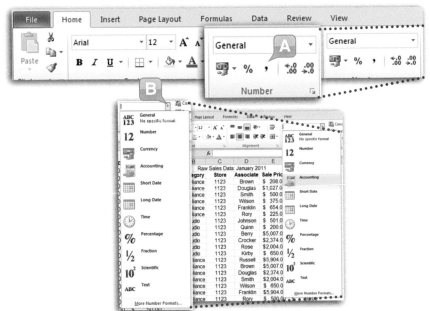

Quickest Click: To quickly perform some of the most common cell formatting tasks, select the cell, row, or column you wish to format, then right-click. The **Currency Combo Button, Percentage Button, Comma Button,** and **Decimal Adjuster buttons** are available in this fly-out menu 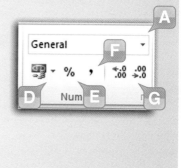 and in the **Number** panel on the **Home** tab :

- **Currency Combo Button:** Click the left half of the button—the half with the symbol—to format the selected cells as currency (100 becomes $100.00). Click the right half of the button—the one with the down arrow—to see more currency and accounting formatting options.
- **Percentage Button:** Click this button to append each number in the selected cells with a % sign.
- **Comma Button:** Click this button to add comma separators to each number in the selected cells and append each number with a decimal point followed by two decimal places (1000 becomes 1,000.00).
- **Decimal Adjuster Buttons:** Click these buttons to add or remove decimal places, one at a time, from numbers (3.14 becomes 3.1 or 3.140).

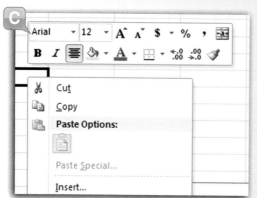

Bright Idea: You can apply formatting to cells before they contain any data. By setting up your formatting before you—or anyone else—enters data into the sheet, you guarantee that formatting will be consistent and make entering the data faster and easier.

12 | Apply Advanced Formatting to Numbers, Dates, and Times

Difficulty: ●○○○

PROBLEM Your company regularly does work for the government, which requires specific date and time formats that are not pre-set options in the **Number** group or the **Number** dropdown.

SOLUTION Use the options in the **Format Cells** dialog box to create the format you desire.

See Also: Convert Text to Numbers; Apply Simple Formatting to Numbers, Dates, and Times

	A	B	C	D	E
1	Salesperson	Order Date	Country	OrderID	Order Amount
2	Bucknell	7/31/2003	USA	10474	$1,249.10
3	Bucknell	8/6/2003	CAN	10248	$440.00
4	Bucknell	8/12/2003	USA	10477	$558.00
5	Bucknell	8/28/2003	CAN	10254	$556.62
6	Bucknell	10/21/2003	CAN	10269	$642.20
7	Bucknell	10/23/2003	USA	10529	$946.00

	A	B	C	D	E
1	Salesperson	Order Date	Country	OrderID	Order Amount
2	Bucknell	Thursday, July 31, 2003	USA	10474	$1,249.10
3	Bucknell	Wednesday, August 06, 2003	CAN	10248	$440.00
4	Bucknell	Tuesday, August 12, 2003	USA	10477	$558.00
5	Bucknell	Thursday, August 28, 2003	CAN	10254	$556.62
6	Bucknell	Tuesday, October 21, 2003	CAN	10269	$642.20

Step-by-Step

Apply a Date Format via the Format Cells Dialog

1. Select the cells to which you want to apply the custom format.

2. On the Home tab in the **Number** group, click the **Format Cells** dialog box launcher **A** to open the **Format Cells** dialog box.

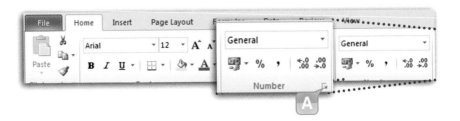

3. Click on the **Number** tab 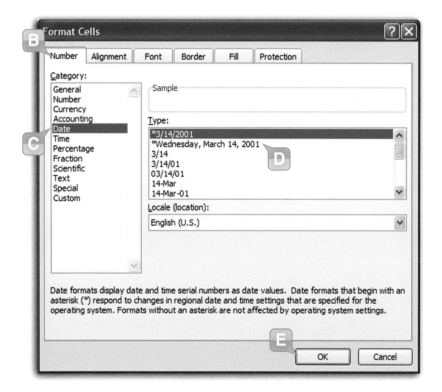.

4. Click on **Date** in the **Category:** pane.

5. Select the specific format you want from the **Type:** combo box.

6. Click the **OK** button.

Step-by-Step

Apply a Time Format via the Format Cells Dialog Box

Use this method to apply custom date or time formatting to your data.

1. Select the cells to which you want to apply the custom format.

2. Open the **Format Cells** dialog box.

3. Click on the **Number** tab.

4. Click on **Time** in the **Category:** pane.

5. Select the specific format you want from the **Type:** combo box. This selection determines how the time is displayed (such as whether midnight is 12:00:00 AM or 00:00:00 AM).

6. Select your location in the **Local (location):** dropdown .

7. Click the **OK** button.

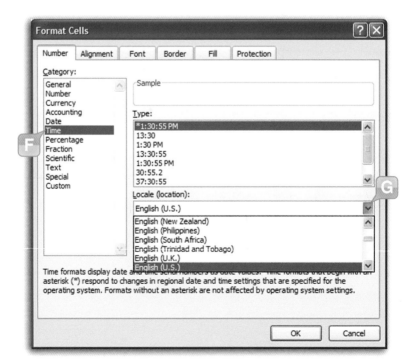

Hot Tip: If you are not in the U.S., or are preparing your sheet for international use, select your location in the **Local (location):** dropdown. This changes the formats available in the **Type:** combo box to match those appropriate to your region.

Bright Idea: Use the **Text** category to convert numbers to text. This selection allows you to begin numbers with zeroes (00934), which number formats will not permit. Once converted, the text numbers should not be used in calculations.

13 | Name a Cell for Use in Formulas and Functions

Difficulty: ⬤◯◯◯

PROBLEM You have a "hardship multiplier" that you add to trainers' per diems when they are required to travel a particular distance, for a certain number of hours per day, or over a set number of days in a row. This value is used in several cells and formulas throughout your sheets. When that value changes, you must locate all the formulas where that multiplier is used.

SOLUTION Create a named cell. Save time and reduce errors by applying a value from a named cell to various formulas and functions instead of applying that number directly to the formula. The cell value can be any length, but by giving it a name, you simplify its use and minimize human error. Updates are made easier as you only have to change the value in one place, not in each relevant cell.

 What Microsoft Calls It: Define a constant

 **Step-by-Step**

Define a Constant by Creating a Named Cell

In this example, a cell is named **_15MinRate** so it can be used in client billing formulas to calculate how much clients should be billed for the time a representative spent with them.

1. Select the cell you want to name Ⓐ.

2. Click the **Define Name** button Ⓑ in the **Define Names** group of the **Formulas** tab to launch the **New Name** dialog box.

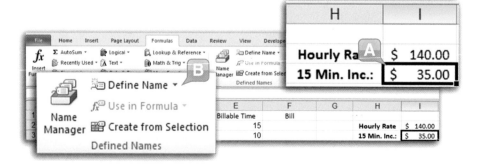

3. In the **Name:** textbox 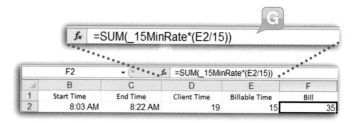 in the **New Name** dialog box, type a name for the cell. The name you choose:

    - Must begin with an underscore.

    - Cannot contain spaces, punctuation, or symbols (except the initial underscore).

    - Cannot be the same as another name in the workbook.

4. Select an option from the **Scope** dropdown menu . The available options are for the name to apply to the whole workbook or to a single sheet.

5. In the **Comment** field , provide a description of the named cell.

6. Click the **OK** button .

7. Use the named cell in a formula .

Bright Idea: You can also apply a name to a whole range of cells, rather than a single cell. To do so, select the range you want to name, and then follow the steps as if you were naming a single cell.

14 Insert Subtotals

Difficulty: ●●○○

PROBLEM You are looking at a list of corporations that donated to your charitable cause throughout a year. The table includes the companies' total donations, dates of donations, industries, and locations. To help you target your campaigns for the next year, you want to find out which industries were most supportive of your cause, which months saw the most donations, and which counties were home to the biggest donors.

SOLUTION Create subtotals to calculate the slices of data you need. Subtotals are functions designed to apply various formulas to columns of data in order to facilitate review and analysis of the table's information.

Subtotals are dynamic in that they adjust instantly based on filters. They are very useful when reviewing a table, as you can make small adjustments to see different perspectives on the information.

Step-by-Step

Create a Subtotal

1. Determine which column you want to subtotal. In this example, the data in Column A will be used to subtotal the data .

	A	B	C	D	E	F
1	Item	Category	Store	Associate	Sale Price	Commission
2	Home Thtr	Audio	1123	Berry	$5,007.00	$ 500.70
3	Stove	Appliance	1123	Berry	$ 225.00	$ 22.50
4	Dishwasher	Appliance	1123	Brown	$ 208.00	$ 20.80
5	LCDTV	Video	3543	Brown	$ 450.00	$ 45.00
6	LCDTV	Video	3543	Brown	$ 798.00	$ 79.80
7	LCDTV	Video	3543	Brown	$1,400.00	$ 140.00
8	Refrigerator	Appliance	1123	Brown	$5,007.00	$ 500.70
9	Home Thtr	Audio	1123	Crocker	$2,374.00	$ 237.40
10	Stove	Appliance	1123	Crocker	$ 501.00	$ 50.10
11	Dishwasher	Appliance	1123	Douglas	$1,027.00	$ 102.70
12	Refrigerator	Appliance	1123	Douglas	$2,374.00	$ 237.40
13	Dishwasher	Appliance	1123	Franklin	$ 654.00	$ 65.40
14	Refrigerator	Appliance	1123	Franklin	$5,904.00	$ 590.40
15	Home Thtr	Audio	1123	Johnson	$ 501.00	$ 50.10
16	Stove	Appliance	1123	Johnson	$ 375.00	$ 37.50
17	Home Thtr	Audio	1123	Kirby	$ 650.00	$ 65.00
18	Stereo	Audio	2354	Kirby	$ 398.00	$ 39.80
19	Stove	Appliance	1123	Kirby	$ 500.00	$ 50.00
20	BluRay	Video	1123	Quinn	$ 399.00	$ 39.90
21	Home Thtr	Audio	1123	Quinn	$ 200.00	$ 20.00
22	Stereo	Audio	1123	Quinn	$ 119.00	$ 11.90
23	Stove	Appliance	1123	Quinn	$ 654.00	$ 65.40
24	Dishwasher	Appliance	1123	Rory	$ 225.00	$ 22.50
25	Refrigerator	Appliance	1123	Rory	$ 500.00	$ 50.00

2. Sort the selected column, Column A in this example, so that the like items in it are grouped 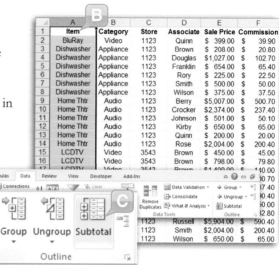. This will let you generate a subtotal for each item group in the column.

3. Click the **Subtotal** button in the **Outline** group on the **Data** tab to launch the **Subtotal** dialog box . This is where you make the selections that generate your subtotals.

4. Select the column you chose to subtotal by from the **At each change in:** dropdown menu . Column A is selected by default, and also happens to be Item, the one used in this example.

5. Select how you would like the data in your selected column subtotaled from the **Use function:** dropdown menu . The selected function is applied to the data in the column(s) you select from the **Add subtotal to:** box. Some of the most common selections are:

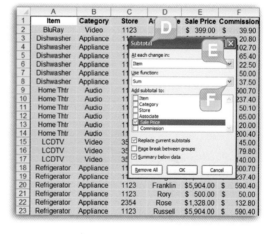

CONTINUE

- **Sum:** Adds the data in the selected column.

- **Count:** Counts and displays the number of rows that contain data in the selected column.

- **Average:** Computes an average from the data in the selected column.

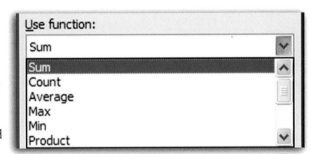

- **Max and Min:** These selections identify the largest or smallest number in the selected column.

6. In the **Add subtotal to:** box , select the columns that will be subtotaled. The default selection is the final column (in this example Column F, Commission). This example also includes Column E, Sale Price.

7. Below the **Add subtotal to:** box are additional options for subtotal layout. Click a checkbox to select the associated option.

  - **Replace current subtotals:** Replaces any existing subtotals on the sheet with the ones you create here.

  - **Page break between groups:** Puts each subtotal on its own printed page.

- **Summary below data:** Places the subtotals at the bottom of each data group and places the grand total at the bottom of the data. If unchecked, the subtotals appear above the data groups and the grand total appears at the top of the data.

8. Click the **OK** button ◯ to generate your subtotals ◯ and grand total ◯.

9. Use the controls in the left margin ◯ to expand or collapse the data for each group. You can also click the control next to grand total to collapse all data. 💡

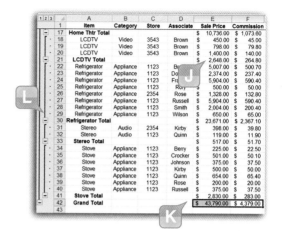

Bright Idea: Once you have completed a subtotal, you can change the subtotal type. That way you can see the total sales and the average commission at the same time. To do so, select the cell that contains the subtotal you'd like to edit ◯. In the **Formula** bar, delete the **function_num** part of the **SUBTOTAL** function ◯. The deleted item is a number that corresponds to a function in the **function_num** dropdown ◯. In this formula, it was nine before it was deleted. Then select a new numbered function from the dropdown.

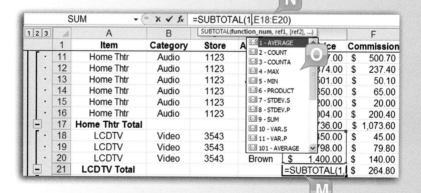

15 Insert a Basic Formula

Difficulty: ●●○○

PROBLEM You want to multiply a sales team's commission percentage by its sales totals.

SOLUTION Use a formula. Writing an Excel formula is exactly like writing a math problem, except the cell coordinates, or addresses, replace some numbers and variables.

Formulas are very useful for performing mathematical calculations between numbers and cells. Once a formula is entered, the cell that contains it appears to only contain the result of the formula's calculation. Clicking on the cell reveals the formula behind the cell's value in the formula bar.

See Also: Copy a Formula to Multiple Cells; Appendix C

	SUM	▾	✕ ✓ ƒx	=C2*D2	
	A	B	C	D	E
1	**Last Name**	**First Name**	**3QSales**	**Comm %**	**Commission**
2	Brown	Angela	$ 2,751.00	6%	=C2*D2
3	Douglas	Serena	$ 3,552.00	4%	$ 142.08
4	Smith	James	$ 726.00	10%	$ 72.60
5	Wilson	Andy	$ 5,041.00	12%	$ 604.92
6	Franklin	Edna	$ 2,547.00	4%	$ 101.88
7	Rory	Hawkins	$ 1,961.00	6%	$ 117.66

Step-by-Step

Enter a Formula

1. Select the cell where you want the calculated total to appear **A**.

2. Click the **Formula Bar B** to place your cursor there.

	E2	▾	ƒx		
	A	B	C	D	E
1	**Last Name**	**First Name**	**3QSales**	**Comm %**	**Commission**
2	Brown	Angela	$ 2,751.00	6%	
3	Douglas	Serena	$ 3,552.00		
4	Smith	James	$ 726.00		
5	Wilson	Andy	$ 5,041.00	12%	
6	Franklin	Edna	$ 2,547.00	4%	
7	Rory	Hawkins	$ 1,961.00	6%	
8	Johnson	Kim	$ 3,275.00	6%	
9	Quinn	Aidan	$ 2,486.00	4%	
10	Berry	Andy	$ 3,051.00	12%	
11	Crocker	Becky	$ 3,462.00	10%	
12	Rose	Amy	$ 1,618.00	6%	
13	Kirby	Bill	$ 1,042.00	6%	

3. Type = in the **Formula Bar** 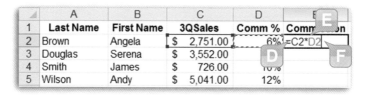.

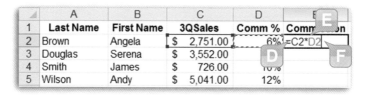

4. Type the first value in your formula **D**, whether that is a cell coordinate or a number.

5. Type an operator **E** between the two values in your formula.

   Common Operators

   + This adds the two values.

   - This subtracts the second value from the first.

   * This multiplies the two values. This is the operator used in the example.

   / This divides the first value by the second.

6. Type the second value in the formula **F**.

7. Press the **ENTER** key on your keyboard to see the result **G**.

 Bright Idea: You can create more complex formulas using additional math rules, such as parentheses, to group various functions.

16 | Copy a Formula to Multiple Cells

Difficulty: ●●○○

PROBLEM You have a standard salary multiplier for overtime hours, which you want to calculate the same way every time. The formula you generate needs to appear along an entire row of data and across several worksheets, but you don't want to type it out each time.

SOLUTION Copy your formula to multiple cells instead of re-typing it. As long as you are using "relative references" (coordinates without "$" markers in them), Excel will adjust the formula each time it copies to apply to the associated data. For example, copying a formula that multiplies cell A1 by B1 to produce a value in C1 can be copied to C2 through C15; and Excel will replace A1 and B1 with A2 and B2 for row 2, A3 and B3 for row 3, etc.

See Also: Insert a Basic Formula; Insert a Basic Function

Step-by-Step

Copy a Formula Using the Fill Handle

Use the **Fill Handle** to copy a formula to several adjacent cells.

1. Select the cell that contains the formula you want to copy **A**.

2. Hover your cursor around the black square in the lower right corner of the cell **B** until your cursor turns into a plus sign **C**; this is the **Fill Handle**.

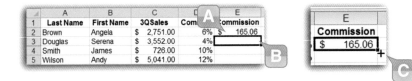

3. Click and hold the left mouse button while dragging the handle to include all cells where you would like the formula to be copied 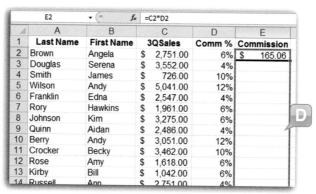.

4. Release the mouse button to populate the cells with the formula E.

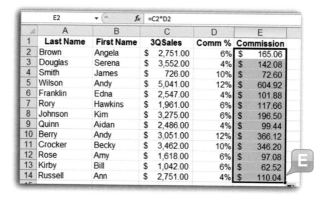

 Hot Tip: Copy the formula to non-adjacent cells by right-clicking the cell that contains the formula, select **Copy,** then right-click the destination cell and choose **Paste**.

Bright Idea: There may be times when you do not want Excel to adjust all or part of the formula for you. For example, if you have a table of standard multipliers that you use in the formula, you might want the same cell to always be used to multiply. You can create what is called an "absolute reference" by inserting a "$" sign to the left of the part of the cell coordinate that you want to stay the same. If you always want to use cell C2, you would write it as "C2".

 STOP

17 Calculate the Difference between Two Times

Difficulty: ●○○○

PROBLEM You need to keep track of how long a particular piece of equipment is used each day. You have the start and stop times for each day's use, but you need to calculate in a useful format what quantity those times represent.

SOLUTION Create a formula to calculate the difference between the start and stop times, then adjust the cell formatting in the **Format Cells** dialog box. Equations that evaluate text, dates, and times all require special handling, and Excel has built-in tools ready to assist you with those evaluations. The actual calculations for times tend to be simple and straightforward, but getting the data to display in a way that is useful and informative is often more challenging. ⚠

Step-by-Step

Calculate the Difference Between Two Times

In this example, the spreadsheet is used to calculate the number of minutes representatives spend talking to each client.

1. Select the cell where the result of the equation, the number of minutes, should appear .

	A	B	C	D
	D2		fx	
1	Client	Start Time	End Time	Client Time
2	Andrews Manufacturing	8:03 AM	8:22 AM	
3	Bridges Building	8:25 AM	8:36 AM	
4	Brown Construction	8:44 AM	9:33 AM	
5	Cook Management	9:36 AM	10:38 AM	
6	Davis Bakeries	9:42 AM	10:46 AM	

2. Type **=C2-B2** Ⓑ to instruct Excel to subtract the Start Time data from the End Time data.

3. Press the **ENTER** key on your keyboard to complete the formula.

	A	B	C	D
	SUM		X ✓ fx =C2-B2	
1	Client	Start Time	End Time	Client Time
2	Andrews Manufacturing	8:03 AM	8:22 AM	=C2-B2
3	Bridges Building	8:25 AM	8:36 AM	
4	Brown Construction	8:44 AM	9:33 AM	
5	Cook Management	9:36 AM	10:38 AM	
6	Davis Bakeries	9:42 AM	10:46 AM	

4. The result may not be what you expected or needed. Below, the result of the equation is displayed in the same HH:MM:SS (hours-minutes-seconds) format as the source cells. To change the appearance, change the formatting.

5. Select Column D, Client Time D.

◢	A	B	C	D
1	Client	Start Time	End Time	Client Time
2	Andrews Manufacturing	8:03 AM	8:22 AM	12:19:28 AM
3	Bridges Building	8:25 AM	8:36 AM	
4	Brown Construction	8:44 AM	9:33 AM	
5	Cook Management	9:36 AM	10:38 AM	
6	Davis Bakeries	9:42 AM	10:46 AM	

6. Click the dialog box launcher for the **Number** group E on the **Home** tab to launch the **Format Cells** dialog box.

7. On the **Number** tab, select **Custom** F in the **Category:** box.

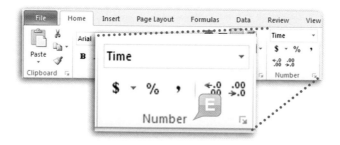

CONTINUE

17 Calculate the Difference between Two Times (continued)

8. In the **Type:** text box, enter **[mm]** 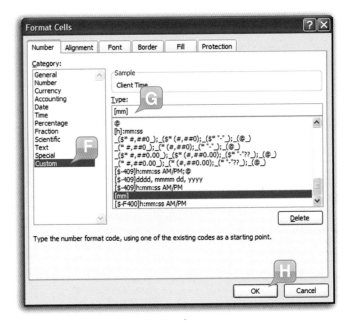. This format tells Excel to display only the minutes.

9. Click the **OK** button.

10. Using the **Fill Handle**, drag the formula to the rest of the cells in the Client Time column and review your results .

B	C	D	
Start Time	**End Time**	**Client Time**	Bil
8:03 AM	8:22 AM	19	
8:25 AM	8:36 AM	10	
8:44 AM	9:33 AM	49	
9:36 AM	10:38 AM	61	
9:42 AM	10:46 AM	63	

Caution: Excel automatically assumes any time you enter is AM unless you specify otherwise.

STOP

18 | Count the Number of Work Days between Two Dates

Difficulty: ●●●○

PROBLEM You want to keep track of how long it takes your shipping department to fulfill an order. You have the dates of when an order is placed and when it is shipped, but you only want to count business days in your reports. ⚠

SOLUTION Excel has a number of built-in date calculation functions to accomplish this and other tasks involving dates.

Step-by-Step

Count the Number of Work Days between Two Dates

In this example, a column is created to track the number of business days that elapse between the time an order is placed and when it ships.

1. Select the cell where you want the number of business days to appear .

	A	B	C	D
1	Order #	Order_Date	Ship_Date	Fulfillme
2	1012	3/5/2011	3/9/2011	
3	1031	3/8/2011	3/15/2011	
4	1125	3/9/2011	3/15/2011	
5	1158	3/15/2011	3/19/2011	

2. Type **=NETWORKDAYS** in the **Formula Bar** Ⓑ. This function tells Excel to do two important things:

   - Count both the start and end days of the date range as part of the total number of days tallied.
   - Ignore any dates that fall on weekends.

3. Follow the instructions in the **Formula Autocomplete** tooltip Ⓒ to add **B2** as the **start_date** value and **C2** as the **end_date** value in the **NETWORKDAYS** formula Ⓓ. ◊

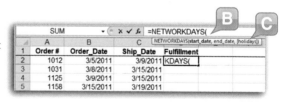

4. Press the **ENTER** key on your keyboard to complete the formula.

5. Use the fill handle to drag the formula to the other cells in the Fulfillment column .

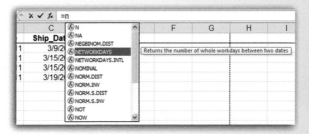

	fx	=NETWORKDAYS(
	C	D
	Ship_Date	**Fulfillment**
	3/9/2011	3
	3/15/2011	6
	3/15/2011	5
	3/19/2011	4

Caution: Be sure you assign a date format to the column where you have dates. Excel's default date format is a number. For example, 7/4/1776 appears as 648858.

Notice that Excel 2010 offers you function suggestions when you begin to type in the formula bar. This gives you a description of the function, offers you a shortcut to typing by hand, and can help ensure that the function is entered correctly.

	C		F	G	H	I
	Ship_Dat	N				
1	3/9/2	NA				
		NEGBINOM.DIST				
1	3/15/2	NETWORKDAYS	Returns the number of whole workdays between two dates			
		NETWORKDAYS.INTL				
1	3/15/2	NOMINAL				
1	3/19/2	NORM.DIST				
		NORM.INV				
		NORM.S.DIST				
		NORM.S.INV				
		NOT				
		NOW				

Hot Tip: Exclude holidays by adding a comma after the end_date value and entering cell addresses that contain dates your company is closed. For example, **=NETWORKDAYS(A2,B2,C2 D2 E2)** would count the number of Monday through Friday days between the dates specified in A2 and B2, less the holiday dates in C2, D2, and E2.

19 Insert a Basic Function

Difficulty: ◯◯◯◯

PROBLEM You bill clients by the quarter hour, rather than by minutes, so you want to take raw time data and round it to the nearest quarter hour to determine how much a client owes you.

SOLUTION A function will allow you to do that with just a few clicks.

Functions are named formula combinations that can be used by name to accomplish advanced calculations with ease. Functions are useful because they allow you to quickly apply mathematical, logical, financial, and text-based formulas to your data.

Using functions is often even easier than using formulas. Excel recognizes when you are using a function and prompts you with correct terminology and formatting to make using them a breeze. A built-in feature called the "Function Wizard" even helps you decide which function you need to achieve the results you are looking for.

Step-by-Step

Insert a Function

This example uses the **ROUNDUP** function to round up from a decimal. The company wants to order supplies in even increments of 100 items. To accomplish this, the Total Needed will need to be rounded up to the nearest 100 items above the required total. In other words, if 1447 items are needed, 1500 should be ordered.

1. Select the cell where you want your rounded-up result to appear .

	A	B	C	D	E	F
1	Items	Beaumont	Regency	Edwardsville	Nee...	Ordered
2	Calendars	239	646	562	1447	
3	Handbooks	256	498	664	1418	
4	Ledgers	47	89	893	1029	
5	Planners	172	88	1087	1347	

2. Type =**ROUND** in the formula bar 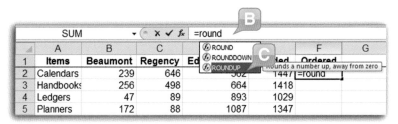.

3. Double-click the **ROUNDUP** option in the **Formula Autocomplete** menu .

4. The **Formula Autocomplete** tooltip shows you what information is required to complete the **ROUNDUP** function—the number to be rounded (number) and the number of decimal places to which that number should be rounded (num_digits).

5. The number in cell E2 (**1447**) is the one that will be rounded up. Click cell E2 to select it.

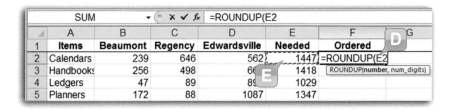

6. Type a comma **G** to separate the number to be rounded from the number of digits to which it should be rounded.

7. Type the number of digits to which the final result should be rounded. In this example, **-2** was selected **H**.

	A	B	C	D	E	F	G
	SUM		▾	✕ ✓ ƒx	=ROUNDUP(E2, -2)		
1	Items	Beaumont	Regency	Edwardsville	Needed	Ordered	
2	Calendars	239	646	562	1447	=ROUNDUP(E2, -2)	
3	Handbooks	256	498	664	1418		
4	Ledgers	47	89	893	1029		
5	Planners	172	88	1087	1347		

- If you select a positive number, such as 1, 2, or 3, a decimal point is added to the end of the number, and the number is rounded up to the number of decimal places, (tenths, hundredths, or thousandths) you selected **I**.

- If you select 0, the number rounds up to the nearest whole number **J**.

- If you enter a negative number, such as -1, -2, or -3, the numbers to the left of the decimal place are replaced with zeroes to the number of digits (tens, hundreds, or thousands) you selected **K**.

	A	B	C
1	Rounded Number	Formula	Result
2	1447.6789	=ROUNDUP(A2,3)	1447.679
3	1447.6789	=ROUNDUP(A3,2)	1447.68
4	1447.6789	=ROUNDUP(A4,1)	1447.7
5	1447.6789	=ROUNDUP(A5,0)	1448
6	1447.6789	=ROUNDUP(A6,-1)	1450
7	1447.6789	=ROUNDUP(A7,-2)	1500
8	1447.6789	=ROUNDUP(A8,-3)	2000

8. Press the **ENTER** key on your keyboard to see the result.

9. Copy the formula to the rest of the cells in the column **L** using the **Fill Handle**.

	F2				fx	=ROUNDUP(E2, -2)	

	A	B	C	D	E	F
1	Items	Beaumont	Regency	Edwardsville	Needed	Ordered
2	Calendars	239	646	562	1447	1500
3	Handbooks	256	498	664	1418	1500
4	Ledgers	47	89	893	1029	1100
5	Planners	172	88	1087	1347	1400
6						

STOP

20 | Use Conditional Functions

Difficulty: ○○○○

PROBLEM You have created a list of customers with the amounts they owe and the amounts they have paid. You need to know how many have not yet paid this month and the amount of outstanding revenue.

Most of the functions you use in your worksheets are designed to yield a single result: You want to add, subtract, multiply, or divide various sheet data. Or you want to check for duplicates or search for particular zip codes. This time, though, you need a formula that changes depending on the data in the cell.

SOLUTION Conditional Functions, functions that typically contain "if" in their names, make formatting logical decisions easy. IF, SUMIF, and COUNTIF are the most commonly used options.

To solve the problem above, you can create fields that count the number of customers who have "$0.00" in their monthly payment column, and apply a SUMIF formula on the monthly payments due column, contingent on "$0.00" being in the monthly payment column.

See Also: Appendix C

Step-by-Step

Use Conditional Functions

In this example, **Column E** (Pmt_Status) is created where **Column D** (Pmts) is evaluated against **Column C** (Due) to determine if the account is current or delinquent. If the payments are greater than or equal to the amount due, the account will be marked "Current," but if the payments are less than the amount due, the account is marked "Delinquent."

1. Select the cell where you want the conditional formula to appear **A**.

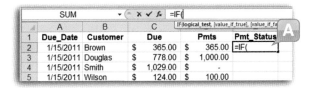

2. Type =**IF** to start the function **B**.

3. Double-click the **IF** option in the **Formula Autocomplete** dropdown that appears **C**.

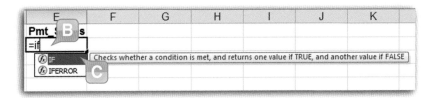

4. The **Formula Autocomplete** tooltip 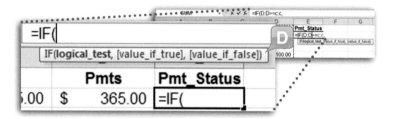 shows you exactly what you need to enter to successfully complete the function.

- **logical_test:** This is the equation that evaluates if the condition is true or false.

- **value_if_true:** This is what the cell contains if the logical test yields an answer of true.

- **value_if_false:** This is what the cell contains if the logical test yields an answer of false.

5. Considering the payments are being evaluated to determine if they are greater than or equal to the amount due, the **logical_test** is **D:D>=C:C** 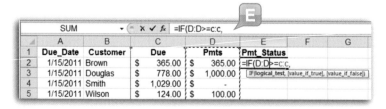. D:D tells Excel to measure each item in column D. The operators > and = describe which measurement will be done. C:C tells Excel what D:D should be compared to.

>: The number on the left side of the symbol is greater than the one on the right. 8>7

<: The number on the left side of the symbol is lesser than the one on the right. 7<8.

>=: The number on the left side of the symbol is greater than or equal to the one on the right. 7>=7, 8>=7.

<=: The number on the left side of the symbol is lesser than or equal to the one on the right. 7<=8, 8<=8.

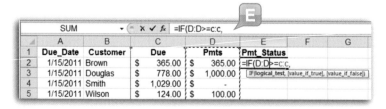

6. The **value_if_true** text displays if the amount in **Column D** (Pmts) is greater than or equal to what is in **Column C** (Due) is **"Current"** 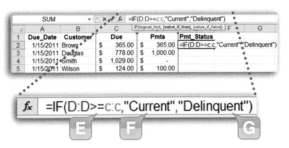. For Excel to understand that it should insert the value as text, it must be enclosed in quotation marks.

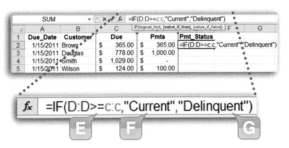

7. The **value_if_false** text displays if the amount in **Column D** (Pmts) is less than the amount in **Column C** (Due) is **"Delinquent"** G.

8. Type **)** to complete the function.

9. Press the **ENTER** key on your keyboard.

10. Verify that the first cell displays the appropriate result, then drag it over a few more cells to test. When you are confident it is working correctly, drag it to the entire column H.

21 | Troubleshoot Formula and Function Errors

Difficulty: ●●○○

PROBLEM Your data just doesn't look correct. There is an error somewhere, but you don't know exactly where the problem is on your worksheet.

SOLUTION Use the **Error Checking** feature. Formulas can become quite complex over time, especially when worksheets have multiple formulas that use one another to produce various results, subtotals, totals, and reports. Excel includes a simple tool to check for and fix errors.

> **What Microsoft Calls It:** Check for errors

Step-by-Step

Perform Error Checking on Formulas

1. You have an error in your calculations when you see the error marker and/or the text **#VALUE!** in a cell .

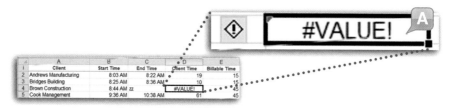

2. Click the **Error Checking** button 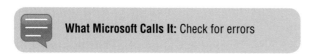 in the **Formula Auditing** group of the **Formulas** tab to launch the **Error Checking** dialog box.

3. If there are errors in your formula, the dialog box lists them 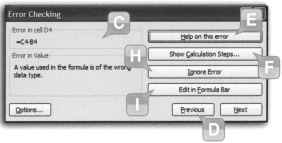, and explains the problem below. Click through the errors found using the **Previous** and **Next** buttons D.

4. For each error, choose one or more actions:

   - Click the **Help on this error** button E to review the Excel Help text on the error.

   - Click the **Show Calculation Steps** button F to view the formula with all source data in place G.

   - Click the **Ignore Error** button H to take no corrective action on any given error.

   - Click the **Edit in Formula Bar** button I to edit the calculation in the formula bar.

5. Once you have viewed and taken action on each error found during the error check, click the **OK** button in the confirmation dialog box to conclude the check.

22 | Find Formulas, Functions, and Cells Connected to a Cell

Difficulty: ⬤⬤⬤◯

PROBLEM You have inherited a worksheet that someone else set up. You want to update the formulas and functions, but you need to know what other, interdependent information will be affected before you make the changes.

For example, you notice that cell A2 contains a value that is used in a formula in cell B2. Because B2 **depends** on cell A2 to calculate its value, you know it is a **dependent** of cell A2. Because a value must be in cell A2 **before** a value can be calculated in cell B2, you know that cell A2 is a **precedent** of cell B2. You do not want to spend hours figuring out every dependent and precedent on your worksheet.

SOLUTION Excel offers a simple way to review which cells are both dependent on and depended upon by other cells.

> **What Microsoft Calls It:** Trace precedents and dependents

Step-by-Step

Find Formulas, Functions, and Cells Connected to a Cell

1. Open your workbook to a sheet you know contains cells that have either precedents or dependents.

2. Select the cell in which you want to check precedents and/or dependents.

3. Click the **Trace Precedents** or **Trace Dependents** button  in the **Formula Auditing** group of the **Formulas** tab. In this example, the dependents for cell B7 are checked.

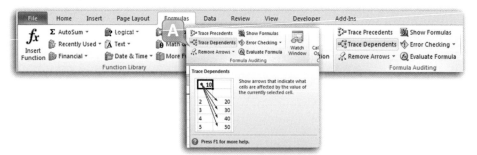

4. Arrows leading from the selected cell extend and point to those cells that use its data in their calculations .

	A	B	C	D	E	F	G	H
1	Month	Days	HCD	Nat. Gas	Product 1	Product 2	Product 3	Total Production
2	Jan	31	2350	173380	334476	265556	1100222	1875984
3	Feb	28	2228	250017	4573992	232422	3304300	8362959
4	Mar	31	305	353722	4830104	353722	4810207	10348060
5	Apr	30	430	118850	3894057	1639043	1156943	6809323
6	May	31	224	90424	3256433	1589756	1063491	6000328
7	Jun	30	52	209123	345876	4077954	1124572	5757577
8	Jul	31	5	201576	407794	1129422	3258498	4997295
9	Aug	31	25	107017	209575	1451356	7209753	8977726
10	Sep	30	425	307678	203948	1039580	2045986	3597617
11	Oct	31	522	132768	4651687	6516587	4654354	15955918
12	Nov	30	468	16875	6543876	5796513	4656731	17014463
13	Dec	31	566	795413	465798	314 1	634684	316584092
14			HCD/Day	Nat. Gas/Day	#1/Day	#2	#3/Day	Production/Day
15			75.806452	5592.903226	10789.5484	8566.32258	35491.032	60515.6129
16			79.571429	8929.178571	163356.857	8300.78571	118010.71	298677.1071
17			9.8387097	11410.3871	155809.806	11410.3871	155167.97	333808.3871
18			14.333333	3961.666667	129801.9	54634.7667	38564.767	226977.4333
19			7.2258065	2916.903226	105046.226	51282.4516	34306.161	193558.9677
20			1.7333333	6970.766667	11529.2	135931.8	37485.733	191919.2333
21			0.1612903	6502.451613	13154.6452	36432.9677	105112.84	161203.0645
22			0.8064516	3452.16129	6760.48387	46817.9355	232572.68	289604.0645
23			14.166667	10255.93333	6798.26667	34652.6667	68199.533	119920.5667

 Hot Tip: Click the **Remove Arrows** button  to clear all precedent and dependent arrows from the screen.

Trace Precedents   Show Formulas
Trace Dependents   Error Checking ▾
Remove Arrows ▾   Evaluate Formula
Formula Auditing

Remove All Arrows

Remove the arrows drawn by Trace
Precedents or Trace Dependents.

❓ Press F1 for more help.

STOP

23 | Calculate Percentages in a PivotTable

Difficulty: ◐◐◐○

PROBLEM You are creating a report that will help prepare your sales team's annual reviews and bonuses for the year. You have a worksheet that shows revenue totals by sales rep, which quickly reveals your top performers. However, you also want to look at those same numbers as percentages to not only give you an idea of who is producing, but to show you what percentage of total revenue they are contributing to the bottom line.

SOLUTION PivotTables do a wonderful job of revealing the important information hidden in your data. Part of what makes them so useful is their flexibility. They can show you your information from a variety of perspective with just a few mouse clicks.

Once you have your data arranged in a PivotTable, you can adjust how you view the information you are analyzing. One way you can adjust the data picture your PivotTable presents is to display numbers and figures as percentages rather than subtotals or grand totals.

See Also: Create a PivotTable

	Sum of Order Amount	Column Labels				
	Row Labels	Sahet	Peterson	Lehoscky	Bucknell	Grand Total
5	Qtr1	18903.29	81283.77	90204.43	22719.01	213110.5
6	Qtr2	18106.66	33357.38	50948.79	6857.67	109270.5
7	Qtr3	14276.39	46821.04	17304.26	16034.62	94436.31
8	Qtr4	21241.29	64301.49	42738.79	23180.95	151462.52
9	Grand Total	72527.63	225763.68	201196.27	68792.25	568279.83

	Sum of Order Amount	Column Labels				
	Row Labels	Sahet	Peterson	Lehoscky	Bucknell	Grand Total
5	Qtr1	3.33%	14.30%	15.87%	4.00%	37.50%
6	Qtr2	3.19%	5.87%	8.97%	1.21%	19.23%
7	Qtr3	2.51%	8.24%	3.05%	2.82%	16.62%
8	Qtr4	3.74%	11.32%	7.52%	4.08%	26.65%
9	Grand Total	12.76%	39.73%	35.40%	12.11%	100.00%

Step-by-Step

Calculate Percentages in a PivotTable

1. Click on any field in your PivotTable.

2. In the **Choose fields to add to report:** selection box of the **PivotTable Field List** panel, click the field  for which you want to calculate percentages.

3. In the **Active Field** group on the **Options** tab of the highlighted **PivotTables** section, click the **Field Settings** button  to launch the **Value Field Settings** dialog box.

 CONTINUE

4. In the **Value Field Settings** dialog box, click the **Show Values As** tab and select the percentage option that matches your needs from the **Show values as** dropdown menu 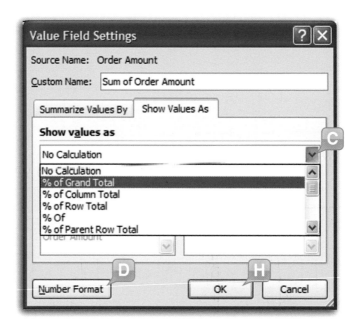. Common selections include:

   - **% Difference From:** This calculation displays each cell's value as a difference between itself and a number you select.

   - **% of:** This calculation displays each cell's value as a percentage of a number you select.

   - **% of Grand Total:**This calculation displays each cell's value as a percentage of all the values or data points in the report.

   - **% of Row Total:** This calculation displays each cell's value as a percentage of the total for its row.

   - **% of column:** This calculation displays each cell's value as a percentage of the total for its column.

5. Click the **Number Format** button D to launch the **Format Cells** dialog box.

6. In the **Format Cells** dialog box, select **Percentage** E from the **Category:** selection box and then use the **Decimal Places** control F to set the number of decimal places you want your percentage to include.

7. Click the **OK** button G in the **Format Cells** dialog box.

8. Click the **OK** button H in the **Value Field Settings** dialog box.

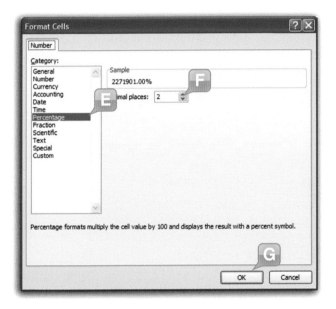

24 Create a PivotTable Calculated Field

Difficulty: ⬤⬤⬤◯

PROBLEM You have a PivotTable that contains fields that tell you how much each of your sales representatives have sold in a given month and how many items comprised each sale. You want to know which sales reps are doing the best job of selling high margin (i.e. more expensive) products.

SOLUTION Create a Calculated Field that divides the sales rep's sales totals by the number of items they have sold.

PivotTables are powerful by themselves, but they can become more powerful yet by adding additional features and functions. Calculated Fields and Calculated Items are two additions that can reveal more about your data than a PivotTable can alone.

When you want to create a new PivotTable field that uses existing PivotTable fields in a formula or calculation, create a calculated field.

Step-by-Step

Create a PivotTable Calculated Field

1. Click on any field in the PivotTable.

	Row Labels ⏷	Sum of Order Amount	Sum of Items in Order
3	**Row Labels** ⏷	**Sum of Order Amount**	**Sum of Items in Order**
4	⊟ **Jul**	**20717.41**	**47**
5	Bucknell	1249.1	2
6	Davis	3474.67	6
7	Fontain	1484	10
8	Peterson	12646.24	27
9	Sahet	1863.4	2
10	⊟ **Aug**	**14226.5**	**50**
11	Bucknell	1554.62	11
12	Davis	3117.28	8
13	Fontain	1360.9	6
14	King	4733.8	8
15	Peterson	2703.9	14
16	Sahet	756	3
17	⊟ **Sep**	**2106.6**	**24**
18	Davis	147	9
19	Peterson	1520.4	12
20	Sahet	439.2	3
21	**Grand Total**	**37050.51**	**121**

2. Click the **Fields, Items, & Sets** button 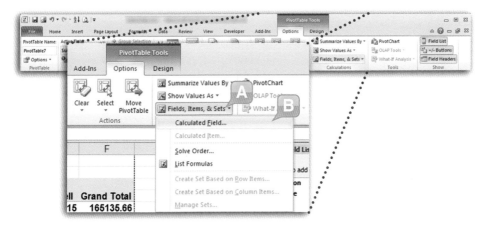 in the **Calculations** group of the **Options** tab in the highlighted **PivotTable Tools** section of the ribbon.

3. Select **Calculated Field** from the **Fields, Items, & Sets** dropdown menu.

4. In the **Insert Calculated Field** dialog box, type a descriptive name for your field in the **Name:** textbox.

5. In the **Formula:** textbox, replace the initial "0" with the fields and operators you want to use in your calculation. In this example, we have added 'Order Amount', a 'forward slash', and 'Items in Order' to show we are subtracting one from the other.

6. Click the **OK** button.

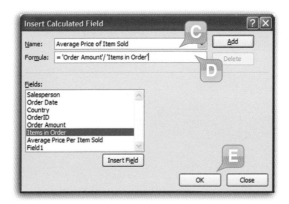

CONTINUE

Create a PivotTable Calculated Field   71

7. Review your new field and data . Note that a column titled Sum of Average Price of Item Sold has been added to the PivotTable.

	Row Labels	Sum of Order Amount	Sum of Items in Order	Sum of Average Price of Item Sold
3	Row Labels ⊤	Sum of Order Amount	Sum of Items in Order	Sold
4	⊟ Jul	20717.41	47	$ 440.80
5	Bucknell	1249.1	2	$ 624.55
6	Davis	3474.67	6	$ 579.11
7	Fontain	1484	10	$ 148.40
8	Peterson	12646.24	27	$ 468.38
9	Sahet	1863.4	2	$ 931.70
10	⊟ Aug	14226.5	50	$ 284.53
11	Bucknell	1554.62	11	$ 141.33
12	Davis	3117.28	8	$ 389.66
13	Fontain	1360.9	6	$ 226.82
14	King	4733.8	8	$ 591.73
15	Peterson	2703.9	14	$ 193.14
16	Sahet	756	3	$ 252.00
17	⊟ Sep	2106.6	24	$ 87.78
18	Davis	147	9	$ 16.33
19	Peterson	1520.4	12	$ 126.70
20	Sahet	439.2	3	$ 146.40
21	Grand Total	37050.51	121	$ 306.20

Hot Tip: Either type a field name in the **Formula:** textbox, or select the field in the **Fields:** box  G and then click the **Insert Field** button H.

Fields:

- Salesperson
- Order Date
- Country
- OrderID
- Order Amount
- Items in Order
- Average Price Per Item Sold
- Field1

Insert Field

25 | Create a PivotTable Calculated Item

Difficulty: ◯◯◯◯

PROBLEM You have a PivotTable that shows you Items and Categories of products, and sales totals for each. You ran a special sale in the month of January and you want to find out what you made on the items that were featured in the sale.

SOLUTION A Calculated Item can give you that information. A calculated item is a new item or category in an existing PivotTable field that uses other items or categories form that same field in a formula or calculation.

See Also: Insert a PivotTable

 Step-by-Step

Create a PivotTable Calculated Item

1. Select an item in your PivotTable.

2. Click the **Fields, Items, & Set**s button 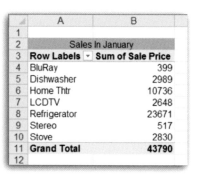 in the **Calculations** group of the **Options** tab in the highlighted **PivotTable Tools** section of the ribbon.

3. Select **Calculated Item** **B** from the **Fields, Items, & Sets** dropdown menu.

	A	B
1		
2	Sales In January	
3	Row Labels ▼	Sum of Sale Price
4	BluRay	399
5	Dishwasher	2989
6	Home Thtr	10736
7	LCDTV	2648
8	Refrigerator	23671
9	Stereo	517
10	Stove	2830
11	**Grand Total**	**43790**
12		

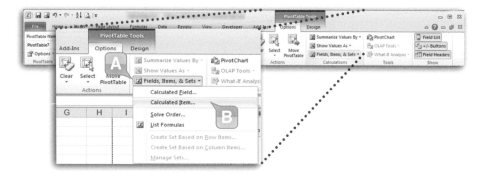

4. In the **Insert Calculated Item** dialog box, type a descriptive name for your item in the **Name:** textbox 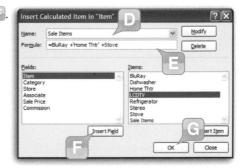.

5. In the **Formula:** textbox, replace the initial "0" with the fields and operators you want to use in the calculation. In this example, we have selected **BluRay, Home Thtr,** and **Stove**, all separated by "plus signs," to show we are adding those fields together.

6. Click the **Insert Field** button.

7. Click the **OK** button.

8. Review your new item .

Hot Tip: You can either type a field name in the **Formula:** textbox, or you can select the field in the **Fields:** box . Double-click an item from the **Items:** box (or click the **Insert Item** button) to insert it.

STOP

26 | Use Data Filters

Difficulty: ●●○○

PROBLEM You are looking at a list of sales records for a particular time period (a day, a week, a month, etc.) There is some data you don't need at the moment, however. You want to examine all but one sales associate, one product, or one store.

SOLUTION Filtering allows you to isolate specific pieces of information for examination. Although there are many ways to do this, filtering is one of the fastest methods.

Step-by-Step

Apply a Data Filter to Your Sheet

1. Click any cell  in the data group you want to filter. **Y**

2. Filter your data.

   - On the **Home** tab, click the **Sort & Filter** button **F** in the **Editing** group.

   OR

   - On the **Data** tab, click the **Filter** button **C** in the **Sort & Filter** group.

	A	A	C	D	E	F
1	**Item**	...ory	**Store**	**Associate**	**Sale Price**	**Commission**
2	Home Thtr	Audio	1123	Berry	$5,007.00	$ 500.70
3	Stove	Appliance	1123	Berry	$ 225.00	$ 22.50
4	Dishwasher	Appliance	1123	Brown	$ 208.00	$ 20.80
5	Refrigerator	Appliance	1123	Brown	$5,007.00	$ 500.70
6	LCDTV	Video	3543	Brown	$ 450.00	$ 45.00
7	LCDTV	Video	3543	Brown	$ 798.00	$ 79.80
8	LCDTV	Video	3543	Brown	$1,400.00	$ 140.00
9	Home Thtr	Audio	1123	Crocker	$2,374.00	$ 237.40
10	Stove	Appliance	1123	Crocker	$ 501.00	$ 50.10
11	Dishwasher	Appliance	1123	Douglas	$1,027.00	$ 102.70
12	Refrigerator	Appliance	1123	Douglas	$2,374.00	$ 237.40
13	Dishwasher	Appliance	1123	Franklin	$ 654.00	$ 65.40
14	Refrigerator	Appliance	1123	Franklin	$5,904.00	$ 590.40
15	Home Thtr	Audio	1123	Johnson	$ 501.00	$ 50.10
16	Stove	Appliance	1123	Johnson	$ 375.00	$ 37.50
17	Home Thtr	Audio	1123	Kirby	$ 650.00	$ 65.00

3. Click the dropdown arrows 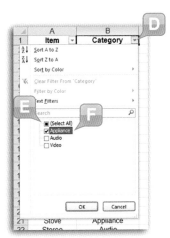 that appear at the top of each column to reveal filtering choices for that column of data.

4. Uncheck the **Select All** box and check the box(es) for the items you want to isolate. In this example **Appliances** was selected in **Column B** Category.

5. Review your selection 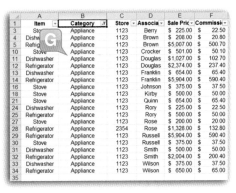.

Options:
- On the **Home** tab, click the **Sort & Filter** button  in the **Editing** group
- On the **Data** tab, click the **Filter** button  in the **Sort & Filter** group.

27 | Highlight Cells Based on Specific Criteria

Difficulty: ●●○○

PROBLEM You are tracking sales revenue by sales associate and you want to use a three-color scale to highlight your lowest sales numbers in red, your highest in green, and your middle in yellow.

SOLUTION Conditional formatting gives you a quick, big-picture view of your sheet so you know where you stand.

Conditional formatting means that the formatting applied to the cells changes dynamically based on conditions. It is used to make at-a-glance spreadsheet and data analysis possible.

	A	B	D
1	**Last Name**	**First Name**	**3Q Sales**
2	Brown	Angela	$ 2,751.00
3	Douglas	Serena	$ 3,552.00
4	Smith	James	$ 2,726.00
5	Wilson	Andy	$ 5,041.00
6	Franklin	Edna	$ 2,547.00
7	Rory	Hawkins	$ 1,961.00
8	Johnson	Kim	$ 3,275.00
9	Quinn	Aidan	$ 2,486.00

Conditional formatting can be based on pre-set rules available via the **Conditional Formatting** dropdown menu; can be customized using Data Bars, Color Scales, and Icon sets; or can be customized based on rules you create from scratch.

	A	B	D
1	**Last Name**	**First Name**	**3Q Sales**
2	Brown	Angela	$ 2,751.00
3	Douglas	Serena	$ 3,552.00
4	Smith	James	$ 726.00
5	Wilson	Andy	$ 5,041.00
6	Franklin	Edna	$ 2,547.00
7	Rory	Hawkins	$ 1,961.00
8	Johnson	Kim	$ 3,275.00
9	Quinn	Aidan	$ 2,486.00
10	Berry	Andy	$ 3,051.00
11	Crocker	Becky	$ 3,462.00
12	Rose	Amy	$ 1,618.00
13	Kirby	Bill	$ 1,042.00
14	Russell	Ann	$ 2,751.00

 What Microsoft Calls It: Conditional Formatting

 **Step-by-Step**

Format a Worksheet Based on Pre-Set Rules

Use this method to quickly apply a conditional format to a selection of cells with numeric data.

1. Select the cells to which you want to apply conditional formatting 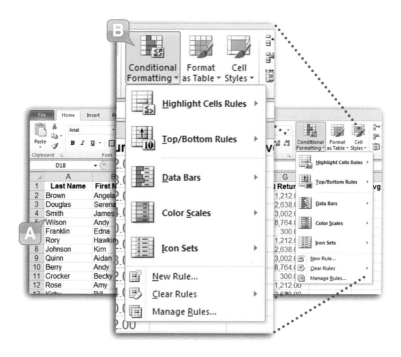.

2. Click the **Conditional Formatting** button **B** in the **Styles** group on the **Home** tab to open the **Conditional Formatting** menu.

3. Select one of the **Rules** options 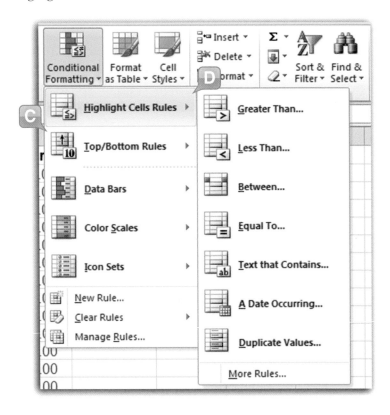.

Highlight Cell Rules :

- **Greater Than/Less Than**: Cells whose values are greater or less than a value you choose are highlighted.

- **Between**: Cells whose values are between two numbers you choose are highlighted.

- **Equal To**: Cells whose values are equal to a number you choose are highlighted.

- **Text that Contains**: Cells that contain text you choose are highlighted.

- **A Date Occurring**: Cells that contain dates matching your criteria are highlighted.

- **Duplicate Values**: Cells that contain values identical to one-another are highlighted.

Top/Bottom Rules 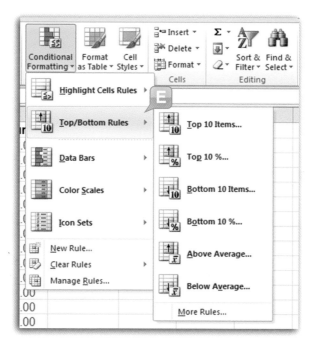:

- **Top Ten/Bottom Ten Items**: Highlights the highest ten or lowest ten values.

- **Top 10%/Bottom 10%**: Highlights the cells that contain values that fall into the highest or lowest 10% of those in your selection.

- **Above/or Below Average**: Establishes an average for your sheet and highlights cells that contain values above or below that average number.

4. In the specialized dialog box that appears for your selected rule, specify any additional criteria and select the formatting that applies to the relevant cells.

5. Click the **OK** button.

28 Use Graphics to Compare Cell Values

Difficulty: ◒◒◒○

PROBLEM You are reviewing a large quantity of data and want a way to find the information you are looking for more easily.

SOLUTION Excel provides several options for graphic and color format that make reviewing your sheet more efficient. At-a-glance formatting options make it easy to find the information you are looking for.

 What Microsoft Calls It: Conditional Formatting

 **Step-by-Step**

Using Data Bars, Color Scales, and Icon Sets

Use this method to highlight cells in a way that provides at-a-glance value comparison between all selected cells.

1. Select the cells to apply conditional formatting.

2. Click the **Conditional Formatting** button in the **Styles** group on the **Home** tab to open the **Conditional Formatting** menu.

3. Select one of the **Rules** options.
   - **Data Bars** Ⓐ: Shades cells with a gradient based on ther comparative values (higher numbers have longer bars).

- **Color Scales** **:** Shades cells with colors based on their comparative values (one color for low values, one for high, and—optionally—one for mid-range).

	A	B	D
1	**Last Name**	**First Name**	**3Q Sales**
2	Brown	Angela	$ 2,751.00
3	Douglas	Serena	$ 3,552.00
4	Smith	James	$ 2,726.00
5	Wilson	Andy	$ 5,041.00
6	Franklin	Edna	$ 2,547.00
7	Rory	Hawkins	$ 1,961.00
8	Johnson	Kim	$ 3,275.00
9	Quinn	Aidan	$ 2,486.00
10	Berry	Andy	$ 3,051.00
11	Crocker	Becky	$ 3,462.00
12	Rose	Amy	$ 1,618.00
13	Kirby	Bill	$ 1,442.00

- **Icon Sets** 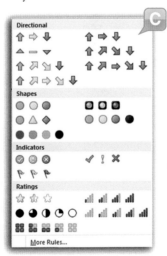**:** Adds an icon to cells based on their comparative values by as many as five measurements.

	A	B	D
1	**Last Name**	**First Name**	**3Q Sales**
2	Brown	Angela	⇨ $ 2,751.00
3	Douglas	Serena	⇨ $ 3,552.00
4	Smith	James	⇨ $ 2,726.00
5	Wilson	Andy	⇧ $ 5,041.00
6	Franklin	Edna	⇩ $ 2,547.00
7	Rory	Hawkins	⇩ $ 1,961.00
8	Johnson	Kim	⇨ $ 3,275.00
9	Quinn	Aidan	⇩ $ 2,486.00

4. In the specialized dialog box that appears for your selected rule, specify any additional criteria and select the formatting to apply to the relevant cells.

Step-by-Step

Create Custom Rules From Scratch

Use this method when none of the pre-set rules and formats meet your conditional formatting needs.

1. Select the cells to which you want to apply conditional formatting.

2. Open the **New Formatting Rule** dialog box .

   • Select **New Rule** from the **Conditional Formatting** dropdown box **B** in the **Styles** group on the **Home** tab.

   • Choose the **More Rules** option **C** from the bottom of any of the other conditional formatting menus. This will take you to the **New Formatting Rule** dialog box with the type of formatting already selected.

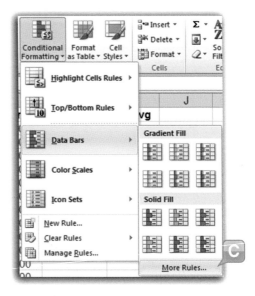

3. Select the type of rule to use as a template from the **Select a Rule Type:** pane 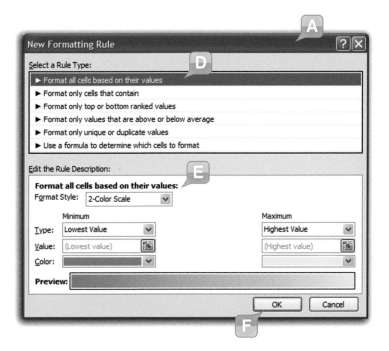.

4. Adjust the rules and formatting options that appear in the **Edit the Rule Description:** pane **E**.

5. Click the **OK** button **F**.

29 Use Sparklines to Display Trends

Difficulty: ◯◯◯◯

PROBLEM You have a year's worth of sales data and you have a PivotTable that displays each sales person's monthly data. You want to show trends in the yearly sales cycle per sales team member in a clear and compact graphical representation without creating a chart on another page.

SOLUTION Use Sparklines. A sparkline is a tiny chart in the background of a cell. When you use a sparkline, you can easily see the relationships between it and its underlying data. And, like other cell formatting, you can copy sparklines to adjacent cells by using the Fill Handle. Another advantage of sparklines is that they are printed as-is when you print a worksheet that contains them, unlike charts that may require special print handling.

Step-by-Step

Insert a Sparkline

1. Select the cells that contain the data you want your sparkline to chart .

◢	A	B	C
1			
2			
3	**Sum of Order Amount**	**Column Labels** ⎌	
4	**Row Labels** ▾	**Sahet**	**Peterson**
5	Jan	4036.34	22387.38
6	Feb	8654.78	29114.29
7	Mar	7414.48	22212.59
8	Apr	5280.16	28704.94
9	May	288	5207.75
10	Jun	5409.5	12899.58
11	Jul	2639.3	24733.18
12	Aug	3996.45	8771.17
13	Sep	9965.36	27103.8
14	Oct	14657.42	17751.56
15	Nov	1132	9574.55
16	Dec	9053.84	17302.89

2. Select the type of sparkline you want from the **Sparklines** panel 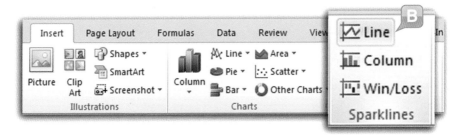 on the **Insert** tab.

3. In the **Create Sparklines** dialog box 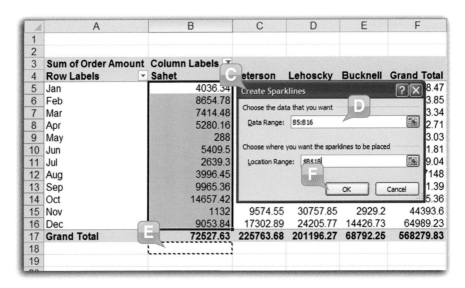, the cell or range you have selected will be filled in the **Data Range:** text box.

4. Type in or click the cell where you want your sparkline to display. A selection box will appear around the destination cell.

5. Click the **OK** button.

6. The sparkline will appear in the position you designated 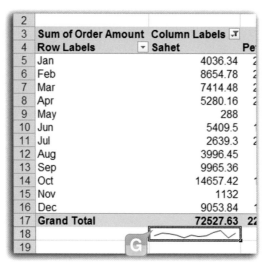 and the **Sparkline Tools** contextual tab  will become available when the cell is selected.

Hot Tip: You can copy a row or column of sparklines using the **Fill Handle**. Select the sparkline you want to copy, then hover over the **Fill Handle** until your curser turns to a cross ⊞. Drag the handle over the cells you want to fill. Sparklines will appear in each of the cells ⒥.

14	Oct			14657.42	17751.56	7634.48	12491.9	52535.36
15	Nov			1132	9574.55	30757.85	2929.2	44393.6
16	Dec			9053.84	17302.89	24205.77	14426.73	64989.23
17	**Grand Total**			**72527.63**	**225763.68**	**201196.27**	**68792.25**	**568279.83**
18								
19								

14	Oct			14657.42	17751.56	7634.48	12491.9	52535.36
15	Nov			1132	9574.55	30757.85	2929.2	44393.6
16	Dec			9053.84	17302.89	24205.77	14426.73	64989.23
17	**Grand Total**			**72527.63**	**225763.68**	**201196.27**	**68792.25**	**568279.83**
18								
19								

14	Oct			14657.42	17751.56	7634.48	12491.9	52535.36
15	Nov			1132	9574.55	30757.85	2929.2	44393.6
16	Dec			9053.84	17302.89	24205.77	14426.73	64989.23
17	**Grand Total**			**72527.63**	**225763.68**	**201196.27**	**68792.25**	**568279.83**
18								
19								
20								

STOP

30 | Customize Your Sparklines

Difficulty: ⬤◯◯◯

PROBLEM You have added sparklines to your worksheet that show a line graph for each sales team member's monthly totals. To get an even better sense of the data, you would like to call out the highest and lowest points on each sparkline. You would also like to change the color schemes to match other documents you are presenting.

SOLUTION Customize your sparklines.

After your sparklines have been created, Excel offers several tools for you to control which value points are shown, set options on the vertical axis, and define how empty values are displayed. You can also change colors, apply styles from Office's pre-loaded style gallery, or apply a custom style that you have saved.

Step-by-Step

---

1. Click on any cell that contains a sparkline to activate the **Sparkline Tools** contextual tab **A**. Click on the **Design** tab **B**. ⬆

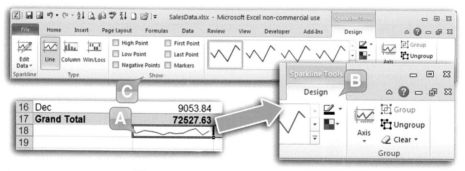

2. In the **Show** group **C** on the **Design** tab, check the points you would like to add to your line.

- **High Point** and **Low Point:** Adds color-coded markers to your sparkline at the highest and/or lowest data point.

- **First Point** and **Last Point:** Adds color-coded markers to the first and last data points.

- **Negative Points:** Adds color-coded markers to negative values.

- **Markers:** Adds a marker at every data point.

Note that the style options in the **Style** group 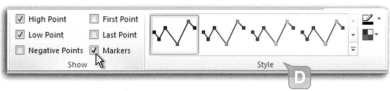 are updated when you make changes in the **Show** group.

3. Review your results **E**. 🔥

14	Oct	14657.42	17751.56	7634.48	12491.9	52535.36
15	Nov	1132	9574.55	30757.85	2929.2	44393.6
16	Dec	9053.84	17302.89	24205.77	14426.73	64989.23
17	**Grand Total**	**72527.63**	**225763.68**	**201196.27**	**68792.25**	**568279.83**
18						
19						

Step-by-Step

Customize the Style or Format of Sparklines

1. Select the sparkline or sparkline group you wish to change **F**.

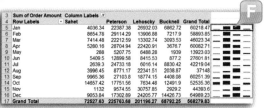

2. In the **Style** group **G** of the **Design** tab, choose the style you want. To see more styles, click the more button **H** in the bottom right corner of the selection box.

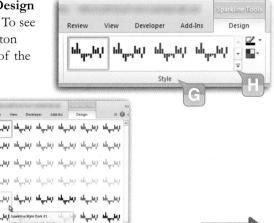

CONTINUE

3. To customize how **High** and **Low Points, First** and **Last Points, Markers** and **Negative Points** are displayed, click on the **Marker Color** button 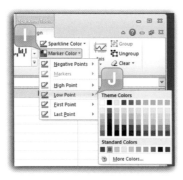 in the **Style** group. Click on the marker you want to change , then choose a color from the fly-out menu.

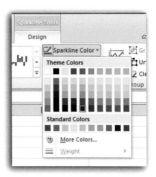

4. To change the color of the line in a line graph, click **Sparkline Color** 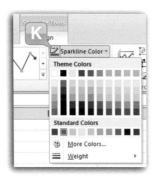 and make your selection from the pull-down menu. To change the thickness of the sparkline, click on **Weight**  and select the point size you want.

5. Review your changes.

D	E	F	G				
oscky	Bucknell	Grand Total					
6932.03	6862.72	60218.47		51.56	7634.48	12491.9	52535.36
3906.88	7217.9	58893.85		74.55	30757.85	2929.2	44393.6
3302.74	3093.53	46023.34		02.89	24205.77	14426.73	64989.23
2420.91	3676.7	60082.71					
6488.28	1939	13923.03		63.68	201196.27	68792.25	568279.83
3415.53	877.2	27601.81					
6016.14	8830.42	42219.04					
2341.51	2038.87	37148					
3774.15	4408.08	60251.39					
7634.48	12491.9	52535.36					
0757.85	2929.2	44393.6					
4205.77	14426.73	64989.23					

Caution: If you select a single cell that is part of a sparkline group, All of the sparklines within that group will be affected when you make formatting changes.

Hot Tip: If your spark lines are too small to see detail, adjust the row height or Column width.

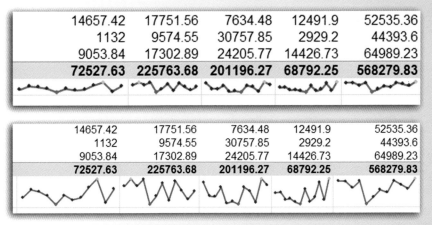

14657.42	17751.56	7634.48	12491.9	52535.36
1132	9574.55	30757.85	2929.2	44393.6
9053.84	17302.89	24205.77	14426.73	64989.23
72527.63	**225763.68**	**201196.27**	**68792.25**	**568279.83**

14657.42	17751.56	7634.48	12491.9	52535.36
1132	9574.55	30757.85	2929.2	44393.6
9053.84	17302.89	24205.77	14426.73	64989.23
72527.63	**225763.68**	**201196.27**	**68792.25**	**568279.83**

31 | Delete a Sparkline or Sparkline Group

Difficulty: ⬤○○○

PROBLEM Your data and your worksheet have changed since you created your sparklines. You need new graphs to represent the data, and it would be easier just to start over than to edit your existing sparklines.

SOLUTION Delete your sparklines. Since sparklines are actually background images in a cell, they will not be removed if you simply select the cell and hit the delete key. You will need to go through the sparklines menu options to remove sparklines that you no longer want.

> 💬 **What Microsoft Calls It:** Clear Sparkline

Step-by-Step

1. Select the sparkline or sparkline group you wish to delete .

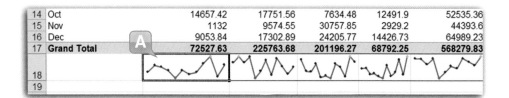

2. In the **Group** group on the **Design** tab, click the **Clear** combo button 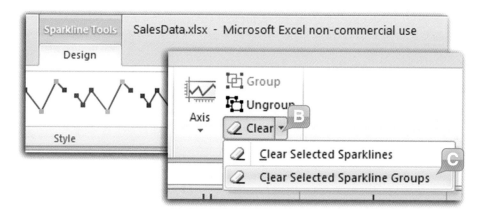 B to remove the selected sparklines. To delete an entire sparkline group, click on the **Clear** dropdown button, then select **Clear Selected Sparkline Groups** C.

32 | Create a PivotTable

Difficulty: ●●●○

PROBLEM You have a table that tracks customer sales data. It includes customer name, payment method, how much was spent, when purchases were made, and what kinds of items were purchased. You want to learn more about your business, such as which categories are most popular, what methods of payment are used to purchase which items, and which days the store sees the highest sales.

SOLUTION PivotTables allow you to take static, dull spreadsheet data and give it meaning. They are among the most powerful data analysis tools available today—and also some of the most under-used.

With a PivotTable, you can see at a glance what you need to do to target credit card customers with specific incentives, time coupon releases to coordinate with the days that are high-volume, or offer buy-one-get-one promotions that pair the items you need to sell more of with those that already perform well.

See Also: Delete a PivotTable; Change How Data Is Displayed in a PivotTable; Group Data Within a PivotTable; Create a PivotTable - Calculated Field; Create a PivotTable - Calculated Item; Create a Chart from Your PivotTable

	A	B	C	D	E	F	G	H
1	Customer	Pmt	Price	Coupon	Item	Category	Prch Date	WkDay
2	Smith	Cash	113.84	0	Stereo	Audio	3/3/2011	Saturday
3	Jones	Cash	82.06	0	Cell Phone	Mobile	3/3/2011	Saturday
4	Wilson	Credit	14.27	0	CD	Mobile	3/3/2011	Saturday
5	Edmonds	Credit	58.52	1	DVD BoxSet	Media	3/3/2011	Saturday
6	Garr	Credit	1838.28	1	PL TV 62"	Video	3/4/2011	Sunday
7	Charles	Debit	12.08	0	Pwr Strip	Accessory	3/4/2011	Sunday
8	Deaton	Debit	96.01	1	Extension	Warranties	3/4/2011	Sunday
9	Rogers	Cash	234.99	1	Zune 80	Audio	3/4/2011	Sunday
10	Ellis	Check	130.6	1	Blu Ray P	Video	3/4/2011	Sunday
11	Katz	Check	69.85	0	17" LT Bag	Accessory	3/4/2011	Sunday

Sum of Coupon	Column Labels ▾		
Row Labels ▾	Sunday	Saturday	Grand Total
⊟ 17" LT Bag	0		0
Accessory	0		0
⊟ Blu Ray P	1		1
Video	1		1
⊟ CD		0	0
Mobile		0	0
⊟ Cell Phone		0	0
Mobile		0	0
⊟ DVD BoxSet		1	1
Media		1	1
⊟ Extension	1		1
Warranties	1		1
⊟ PL TV 62"	1		1
Video	1		1
⊟ Pwr Strip	0		0
Accessory	0		0
⊟ Stereo		0	0
Audio		0	0
⊟ Zune 80	1		1
Audio	1		1
Grand Total	4	1	5

Step-by-Step

Create a PivotTable

1. Select the data to include in your PivotTable, including column headers.

2. Click on the **Insert** tab and select **PivotTable** from the **Tables** panel to open the **Create PivotTable** dialog **A**.

3. Select:

    • Data you want to analyze (the default is your selected cells).

    • Where to place the PivotTable.

If you choose to place it on your current sheet, you need to select the cells where you'd like it to sit **B**.

4. Click the **OK** button **C**.

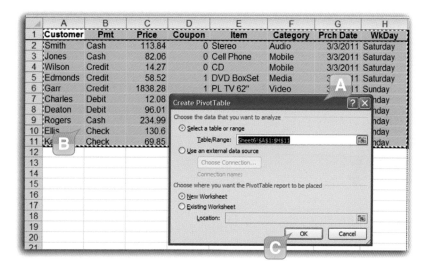

CONTINUE

This opens the **PivotTable Field List** pane 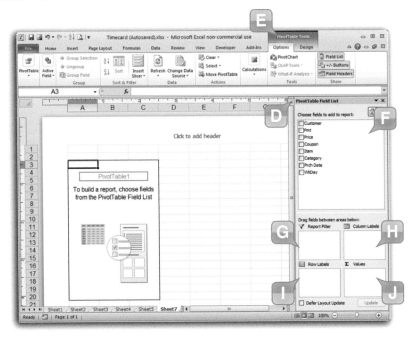 D and makes the **PivotTable Tools** tabs E available for use.

5. In the **Choose fields to add to report:** window F of the **PivotTable Field List** panel, check the fields to include in the PivotTable.

6. Click and drag fields to display in the following boxes:
   - **Report Filter:** Fields dragged into this box control what data is filtered on in the PivotTable G.
   - **Column Labels:** Fields dragged here will be displayed as columns H.
   - **Row Labels:** Fields dragged here will be displayed as rows I.
   - $\sum$ **Values:** Fields dragged here will display as data J.

In our example data, your PivotTable can now show you how many coupons were used on Saturday and Sunday 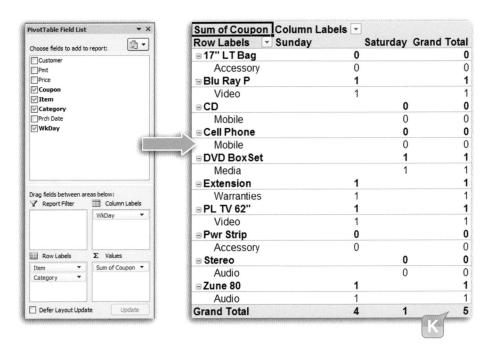, and what items the coupons were used for.

Sum of Coupon	Column Labels		
Row Labels	Sunday	Saturday	Grand Total
⊟ 17" LT Bag	0		0
Accessory	0		0
⊟ Blu Ray P	1		1
Video	1		1
⊟ CD		0	0
Mobile		0	0
⊟ Cell Phone		0	0
Mobile		0	0
⊟ DVD BoxSet		1	1
Media		1	1
⊟ Extension	1		1
Warranties	1		1
⊟ PL TV 62"	1		1
Video	1		1
⊟ Pwr Strip	0		0
Accessory	0		0
⊟ Stereo		0	0
Audio		0	0
⊟ Zune 80	1		1
Audio	1		1
Grand Total	4	1	5

Bright Idea: Change the fields in the PivotTable for a fresh look at your data. Any time you wish to change your PivotTable, click on any cell in the PivotTable to open the **PivotTable Tools** contextual tab. Make sure the **Field List** button in the **Show** panel on the **Options** tab is selected, then make your changes in the **PivotTable Field List** panel.

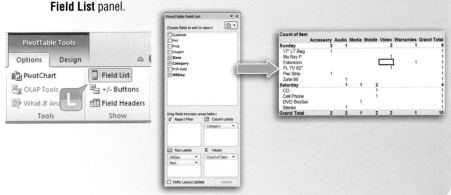

33 Delete a PivotTable

Difficulty:

PROBLEM The data and format of an existing PivotTable is no longer useful. You want to start over from scratch.

SOLUTION Delete the entire table.

Step-by-Step

Delete a PivotTable

1. Click anywhere in the PivotTable to be deleted.

2. In the **PivotTable Tools** contextual tab **A**, click the **Options** tab **B**.

3. In the **Actions** group **C**, click the **Select** button **D**.

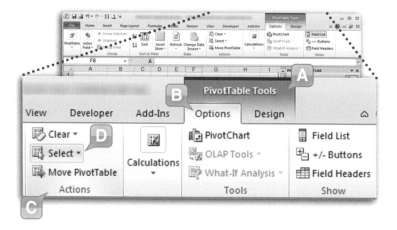

4. On the context menu that appears, choose **Entire PivotTable** 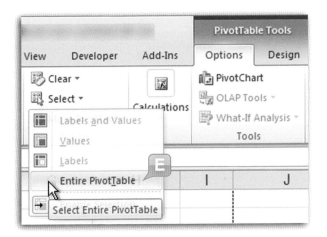.

5. Press the **Delete** key on your keyboard.

Hot Tip: When the data behind a PivotTable is updated or changed, you don't need to delete your table and re-create it to reflect the new data. Instead, refresh the table to show the new information. To do so, click on any cell in the PivotTable to reveal the **PivotTable Tools** contextual tab. On the **Options** tab, click the **Refresh** button in the **Data** group.

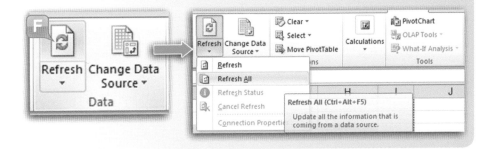

STOP

Difficulty: ◐◐◐◐

PROBLEM You want to change the way that data is displayed in your PivotTable. In your table (below), the number of coupons used in any given transaction is listed in the Coupon column **A**. An empty cell indicates no coupon was used. When you create your PivotTable, by default, numeric values will use the **SUM** function to add values, and text or empty cells will use the **COUNT** function to count the *number* of values. **A** The **COUNT** function **B** default will tell you how many customers used coupons, but it won't tell you how *many* coupons were used in total.

SOLUTION Change the function to summarize your data by **SUM** **C** instead of **COUNT**. Changing the function to **SUM** will provide you with the totals you need.

	A	B	C	D	E	F	G	H
1	Customer	Pmt	Price	Coupon	Item	Category	Prch Date	WkDay
2	Smith	Cash	113.84	2	Stereo	Audio	3/3/2011	Saturday
3	Jones	Cash	82.06	1	Cell Phone	Mobile	3/3/2011	Saturday
4	Wilson	Credit	14.27	3	CD	Mobile	3/3/2011	Saturday
5	Edmonds	Credit	58.52	1	DVD BoxSet	Media	3/3/2011	Saturday
6	Garr	Credit	1838.28	3	PL TV 62"	Video	3/4/2011	Sunday
7	Charles	Debit	12.08		Pwr Strip	Accessory	3/4/2011	Sunday
8	Deaton	Debit	96.01		Extension	Warranties	3/4/2011	Sunday
9	Rogers	Cash	234.99		Zune 80	Audio	3/4/2011	Sunday
10	Ellis	Check	130.6	1	Blu Ray P	Video	3/4/2011	Sunday
11	Katz	Check	69.85		17" LT Bag	Accessory	3/4/2011	Sunday

	Count of Coupon	Sum of Price
Charles		12.08
Deaton		96.01
Edmonds	1	58.52
Ellis	1	130.6
Garr	1	1838.28
Jones	1	82.06
Katz		69.85
Rogers		234.99
Smith	1	113.84
Wilson	1	14.27
Grand Total	6	2650.5

	Sum of Coupon	Sum of Price
Charles		12.08
Deaton		96.01
Edmonds	1	58.52
Ellis	1	130.6
Garr	3	1838.28
Jones	1	82.06
Katz		69.85
Rogers		234.99
Smith	2	113.84
Wilson	3	14.27
Grand Total	11	2650.5

What Microsoft Calls It: Summarize Values By

 **Step-by-Step**

Change How PivotTable Data Is Displayed

1. Right-click any cell in a column where you would like to change the way data is displayed.

2. In the context menu that appears, click **Summarize Values By** 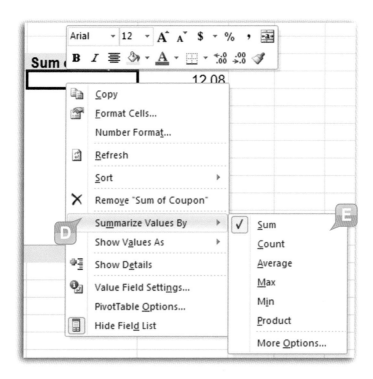 and click the data summary option that best meets your needs.

- **Sum:** Sums the values of all cells in the range 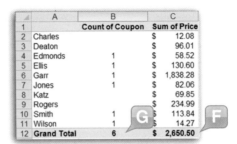.

- **Count:** Displays the total number of cells in the selected range that contain a value .

	A	B	C
1		**Count of Coupon**	**Sum of Price**
2	Charles		$ 12.08
3	Deaton		$ 96.01
4	Edmonds	1	$ 58.52
5	Ellis	1	$ 130.60
6	Garr	1	$ 1,838.28
7	Jones	1	$ 82.06
8	Katz		$ 69.85
9	Rogers		$ 234.99
10	Smith	1	$ 113.84
11	Wilson	1	$ 14.27
12	**Grand Total**	**6**	**$ 2,650.50**

- **Average:** Calculates the average of the values of the cells in the selected range .

	A	B	C
1		**Count of Coupon**	**Average of Price**
2	Accessory		$ 40.97
3	Audio	1	$ 174.42
4	Media	1	$ 58.52
5	Mobile	2	$ 48.17
6	Video	2	$ 984.44
7	Warranties		$ 96.01
8	**Grand Total**	**6**	**$ 265.05**

- **Max:** Displays the highest value in the selected range of cells .

	A	B	C
1		**Count of Coupon**	**Max of Price**
2	Accessory		$ 69.85
3	Audio	1	$ 234.99
4	Media	1	$ 58.52
5	Mobile	2	$ 82.06
6	Video	2	$ 1,838.28
7	Warranties		$ 96.01
8	**Grand Total**	**6**	**$ 1,838.28**

- **Min:** Displays the lowest value in the selected range of cells 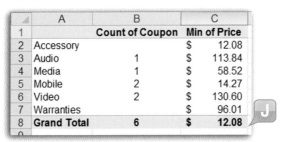.

	A	B	C
1		**Count of Coupon**	**Min of Price**
2	Accessory		$ 12.08
3	Audio	1	$ 113.84
4	Media	1	$ 58.52
5	Mobile	2	$ 14.27
6	Video	2	$ 130.60
7	Warranties		$ 96.01
8	**Grand Total**	6	$ 12.08

- **Product:** Displays the product obtained when each value in the range is multiplied by the next 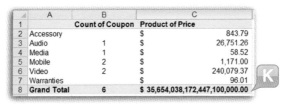.

	A	B	C
1		**Count of Coupon**	**Product of Price**
2	Accessory		$ 843.79
3	Audio	1	$ 26,751.26
4	Media	1	$ 58.52
5	Mobile	2	$ 1,171.00
6	Video	2	$ 240,079.37
7	Warranties		$ 96.01
8	**Grand Total**	6	$ 35,654,038,172,447,100,000.00

- **More Options:** Launches the **Value Field Settings** dialog box , which provides access to additional options and settings.

 Caution: The **COUNT** function counts any value that is present in a cell, even if that value is "0." In the Coupon example, if the coupon cells were filled with the number "0," you would get inaccurate results. The tally would show that coupons were used in every transaction (because a value—any value—is present in the cell.

35 | Group Data Within a PivotTable

Difficulty: ●●●○

PROBLEM You are looking at twenty years of data broken down by day, month, and year. The sheer quantity of data you are reviewing makes it difficult to isolate the information you need. You would rather analyze the data by month **A**, quarter **B**, year, and maybe even decade.

SOLUTION Group the data. Grouping data doesn't eliminate the more detailed information, it merely collapses it into units that can be reviewed or expanded to show the original components. Once grouped, each group receives its own dropdown menu that allows you to expand or collapse the detail.

See Also: Create a PivotTable

Sum of Order Amount	Column Labels			
Row Labels	Sahet	Peterson	Lehoscky	Bucknell	Grand Total
⊟ USA		225763.68	201196.27		426959.95
7/11/2003		3597.9			3597.9
7/12/2003		1552.6			1552.6
7/15/2003			654.06		654.06
7/16/2003			1444.8		1444.8
7/17/2003			517.8		517.8
7/22/2003		1119.9			1119.9
7/25/2003		100.8			100.8
7/29/2003		1504.65			1504.65
7/30/2003		448			448
7/31/2003			346.56		346.56
8/6/2003		3536.6			3536.6
8/12/2003			2037.28		2037.28
8/21/2003		241.9			241.9
8/23/2003			1414.8		1414.8
8/27/2003		1170.37			1170.37

A

Sum of Order Amount	Column Labels			
Row Labels	Sahet	Peterson	Lehoscky	Bucknell	Grand Total
⊟ USA		225763.68	201196.27		426959.95
Jan		22243.03	28693.32		50936.35
Feb		39644.71	35656.39		75301.1
Mar		19396.03	25854.72		45250.75
Apr		17383.87	18093.96		35477.83
May		10569.34	14180.45		24749.79

B

Sum of Order Amount	Column Labels			
Row Labels	Sahet	Peterson	Lehoscky	Bucknell	Grand Total
⊟ USA		225763.68	201196.27		426959.95
Qtr1		81283.77	90204.43		171488.2
Qtr2		33357.38	50948.79		84306.17
Qtr3		46821.04	17304.26		64125.3
Qtr4		64301.49	42738.79		107040.28

 **Step-by-Step**

Group Data in a PivotTable

1. Right-click any cell in the row or column that contains the data you want to group 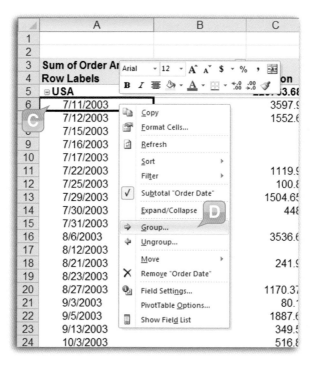.

2. Click the **Group** option in the context menu.

3. In the **Grouping** dialog box :

- Adjust the values in **Auto** textboxes (in the illustration below, the parameters are dates because the data being grouped is dates) *or* uncheck the **Auto** checkboxes to ignore these fields.

- Select an option from the **By** selection box to group your data by that increment.

4. Review your data, now grouped in the way you identified ⓘ.

Sum of Order Amount	Column Labels			
Row Labels	Sahet	Peterson	Lehoscky	Bucknell	Grand Total
⊟ USA		225763.68	201196.27		426959.95
Jan		22243.03	28693.32		50936.35
Feb		39644.71	35656.39		75301.1
Mar		19396.03	25854.72		45250.75
Apr		17383.87	18093.96		35477.83
May		10569.34	14180.45		24749.79
Jun		5404.17	18674.38		24078.55
Jul		13119.54	4840.18		17959.72
Aug		22083.11	5191.83		27274.94
Sep		11618.39	7272.25		18890.64
Oct		24473.08	12875.89		37348.97
Nov		12075.71	9775.23		21850.94
Dec		27752.7	20087.67		47840.37

STOP

36 Find a Value from Another Table

Difficulty: ◐◐◐◯

PROBLEM   Your organization receives money from donors to support its various charitable projects. You need to find out how much money a given donor gave you last year. Because there are thousands of donors in your system, and because each donor record contains dozens of pieces of information (name, address, phone number, preferred projects, donation history, etc.), scrolling through pages of information to find the data would take hours.

SOLUTION   **VLOOKUP** is a powerful tool that allows you to identify a collection of data to search, look through one column for a value, and return the value in a different column for that row. A **VLOOKUP** for donor Mark Smith returning the YTD_Donations column data will make your process much faster.

 What Microsoft Calls It: VLOOKUP

Step-by-Step

Conduct a VLOOKUP Query

In this example, a Donor Lookup field is created in which a donor's name can be entered and the cell containing the VLOOKUP formula returns last year's total donations for that member.

1.   Open a worksheet in which you want to create a **VLOOKUP** field.

2. In this example, a label field is created 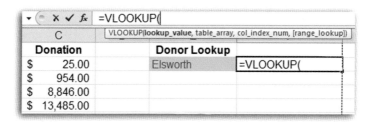, and the field where the name can be entered is highlighted green for clarity. The field where the donor's name can be entered is E2, and the **VLOOKUP** resides in F2.

	A	B	C	D	E
1	**Level**	**Donor**	**Donation**		**Donor Lookup**
2	Member	Gayle	$ 25.00		Elsworth
3	Member	Morton	$ 954.00		
4	Honor	Elsworth	$ 8,846.00		
5	Bronze	Grandy	$ 13,485.00		

3. Enter a sample value in the field that is referenced by the **VLOOKUP** function. It should be a value near the top of the data list that quickly shows whether or not the formula is entered correctly when you complete it. In this case, Elsworth was entered.

4. Select the cell where the VLOOKUP formula will reside. In this example, that is cell F2.

▼	× ✓ *fx*	=VLOOKUP(	
		VLOOKUP(lookup_value, table_array, col_index_num, [range_lookup])	
C		**Donor Lookup**	
Donation			
$ 25.00		Elsworth	=VLOOKUP(
$ 954.00			
$ 8,846.00			
$ 13,485.00			

CONTINUE

5. Type **=VLOOKUP(** in the **Formula Bar.** Complete the formula as prompted by the **Formula Autocomplete Tooltip** B.

- The **lookup_value** C is the cell where the searched term is entered. In this example, cell E2 is where the donor's name is entered ⚠.

- The **table_array** D should be the area of data that is searched for the lookup value and the returned value (in this case, the donation amount). In this example, that is cells B2 (the top value-containing cell in the Donor column) through C21 (the bottom value-containing cell in the Donation column).

- The **col_index_num** E is the number of the column in the selected array searched for the returned value. Column C is the one searched, and while it is Column 3 in your table (counting from left to right), it is only Column 2 of the array you identified for the VLOOKUP. **2** (for Column 2) is entered here.

- The **range_lookup value** F is either TRUE or FALSE. Entering a value of TRUE requires the searched column (the donor column in this example) to be in ascending order, and causes Excel to search for an approximate match. A selection of FALSE eliminates the ascending order requirement but searches only for an exact match. In this example, FALSE is selected.

6. Close the parentheses in the formula.

7. Press the **ENTER** key on your keyboard.

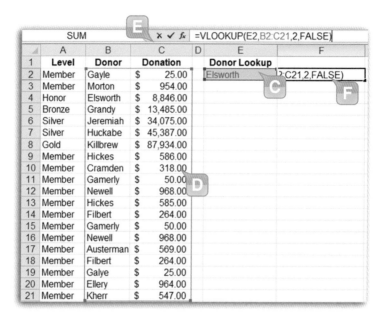

8. Review the result .

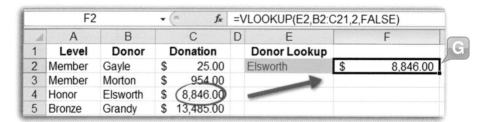

Caution: If you plan to apply your VLOOKUP formula to multiple cells, make sure your table array arguments are absolute references.

37 | Create a Slicer

Difficulty: ●●●○

PROBLEM　You have a PivotTable that shows monthly totals for every sales person in your team. However, the large size of your team makes it hard to compare performance from person to person.

SOLUTION　Create a Slicer to quickly view only the team members you want to study at any given moment.

Introduced in Excel 2010, a Slicer is a filtering component that contains a set of buttons which enables you to quickly filter your PivotTable data without having to open dropdown lists. A Slicer is usually associated with the PivotTable in which it is created, but it can also be stand-alone or associated with other PivotTables.

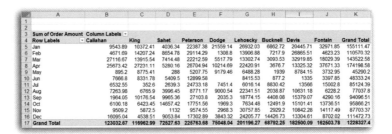

Sum of Order Amount	Column Labels									
Row Labels	Callahan	King	Sahet	Peterson	Dodge	Lehoscky	Bucknell	Davis	Fontain	Grand Total
Jan	9543.89	10372.41	4036.34	22387.38	21559.14	26932.03	6862.72	20445.71	32971.85	155111.47
Feb	4671.69	14207.24	8654.78	29114.29	1308.8	13906.88	7217.9	26865.51	4623.23	110570.32
Mar	27116.67	13915.54	7414.48	22212.59	5517.79	13302.74	3093.53	32919.85	18029.39	143522.58
Apr	25673.42	27231.11	5280.16	28704.94	10214.69	22420.91	3676.7	13325.32	37671.33	174198.58
May	895.2	8775.41	288	5207.75	9179.46	6488.28	1939	8784.15	3732.95	45290.2
Jun	7666.8	8331.78	5409.5	12899.58		8415.53	877.2	1335	3397.85	48333.24
Jul	6532.55	352.6	2639.3	24733.18	7451.4	6016.14	8830.42	13566	15002.8	85124.39
Aug	7263.98	6785.9	3996.45	8771.17	9000.54	22341.51	2038.87	10631.18	6228.2	77037.8
Sep	1984.05	10176.54	9965.36	27103.8	2035.3	18774.15	4408.08	15379.07	4290.16	94096.51
Oct	6100.18	6423.45	14657.42	17751.56	1969.3	7634.48	12491.9	15101.41	13736.51	95866.21
Nov	9509.2	5872.5	1132	9574.55	2968.3	30757.85	2929.2	10842.28	14117.49	87703.37
Dec	16095.04	4538.51	9053.84	17302.89	3843.32	24205.77	14426.73	13304.61	8702.02	111472.73
Grand Total	123032.67	116962.99	72527.63	225763.68	75048.04	201196.27	68792.25	182500.09	162503.78	1228327.4

📖 Step-by-Step

1. Click on any cell within the PivotTable for which you want to create a slicer. This will activate the **PivotTable Tools** contextual tab.

2. In the **Sort & Filter** group in the **Options** tab, click on the **Insert Slicer** Ⓐ combo button.

analyze

3. In the **Insert Slicers** dialog box, select the PivotTable fields for which you want to create a slicer.

4. Click the **OK** button. A slicer will be created on the same worksheet for every field that you selected.

5. In the slicer window, click on any item on which you want to filter. If you want to view more than one item at a time, hold the CTRL key and click multiple items.

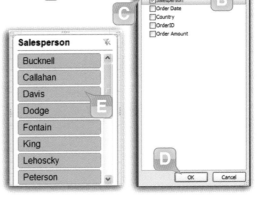

Bright Idea: Your slicer panel can be formatted to match the style of your data and PivotTable. Click the style that you want in the **Slicer Styles** group, on the **Options** tab under the **Slicer Tools** contextual tab. To see all styles available, click the **More** button on the **Slicer Styles** selection box.

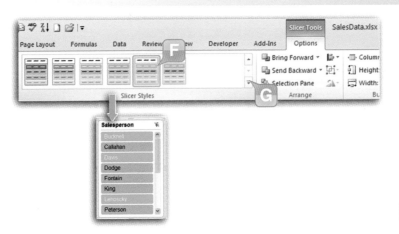

STOP

Create a Slicer   115

38 Delete a Slicer

Difficulty: ●○○○

PROBLEM Your data and your PivotTable have changed since you created your slicers, and your manager has asked for a new set of reports based on the new information. You do not need the old slicer any longer.

SOLUTION Delete the slicer.

Since sparklines are actually background images in a cell, they will not be removed if you simply select the cell and hit the delete key. You will need to go through the sparklines menu options to remove sparklines that you no longer want.

Step-by-Step

1. Click anywhere on the slicer pane, then hit the **Delete** key.

   OR

2. Right-click on the slicer pane and select **Remove "slicername"** [A].

39 Find the Tab that Allows Access to Macros and VBA

Difficulty: ○○○○

PROBLEM You open a workbook that contains macros and see a Security Alert message. You can't find the **Macro Dialog Box** and you see that all VBA content is disabled by the default version of the program.

SOLUTION Enable the **Developer** tab. If you frequently use workbooks and worksheets that include macros, or if you are an advanced user accustomed to utilizing advanced macro and VBA functions, you may find the default setting in Excel 2007 somewhat limiting. The **Developer** tab is where you will change these settings.

> **What Microsoft Calls It:** Enabling the Developer Tab, Enabling VBA, Enabling Visual Basic for Applications

---

 **Step-by-Step**

Enable the Developer Tab

1. Use this solution to record macros, or if you routinely access and edit workbooks that contain macros.

2. Click the **File** tab.

3. Click the **Excel Options** button.

4. Click the **Customize Ribbon** button.

5. Click the **Developer** checkbox **A** so it is checked in the **Main Tabs** box.

6. Click the **OK** button.

Caution: Be careful when you modify your macro security settings. Macros are very powerful. Enabling the **Developer** tab opens your system to potential security hazards.

Quickest Click: Enable Macros
Use this solution to enable macros in a particular trusted workbook. If you receive a **Security Warning** B on your **Message Bar** C when opening a macro-enabled workbook, click the **Enable content** radio button D to enable macros in this workbook only.

If you want more options or to find out more about the Active Content contained in the workbook, go to the **Backstage View** by clicking the **File** tab. Make sure the **Info** button is selected to see the **Security Warning** area E. Click on the down arrow on the **Enable Content** button to enable all the Active Content or access **Advanced Options** F.

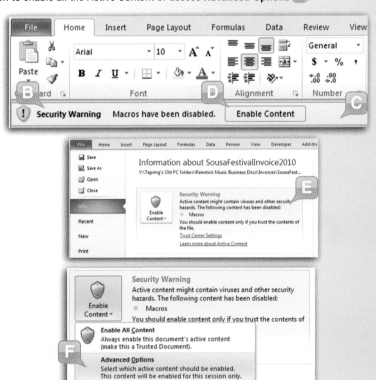

40 | Record a Macro

Difficulty: ⬤◯◯◯

PROBLEM You receive a spreadsheet every week from a reseller that markets your products. You perform the same changes weekly to adjust the format of the sheet to your company's standards. You also run a series of custom calculations to help you evaluate the reseller's performance. These calculations involve adding a formula to the same columns and cells every week. You want a way to make these repetitive tasks easier and faster.

SOLUTION Record a macro. Macros automate repetitive tasks to speed up and streamline work in Excel. They are collections of commands that perform pre-determined actions in your worksheet. Macros can either be recorded (Excel tracks and saves your actions) or programmed (written in VB—Visual Basic—code in a special editor.)

Macros can be used for a number of different functions. You can record a series of actions that sets up your spreadsheet to look a certain way or organizes your data in a particular fashion. You can record the actions, save it as a macro, and then make those changes with a single click going forward. Macros can also be used to run a series of calculations on a collection of data. If you always prepare a report by multiplying the items in a certain column by the corresponding items in the next column, you can set up a macro that performs that action each time you need it done with one keystroke.

See Also: Find the Tab that Allows Access to Macros and VBA

Step-by-Step

Record a Macro

This macro takes raw sales data from a report and converts it into user-friendly information. The report used in this example has three columns.

- Column A contains the number of the store that made each sale.

- Column B contains the date each sale was made, but the date is expressed in the native Microsoft Excel numeric format, meaning that it is just a series of seemingly random numbers.

- Column C contains the amount of each sale, but the prices are formatted as numbers rather than currency.

	A	B	C
1	Store Number	Transaction Date	Amount
2	1123	39845	15
3	1123	39085	3
4	1123	39085	2.75
5	2345	39085	22
6	2345	39805	27
7	2345	39845	5.25
8	2345	39085	3

The goal in this example is to create a macro that converts the Transaction Date data to a standard date format and the Amount to dollars.

1. Make sure the **Developer** tab is enabled. The tab is enabled if it is visible on the ribbon.

2. Click the **Record Macro** button A in the **Code** group on the **Developer** tab.

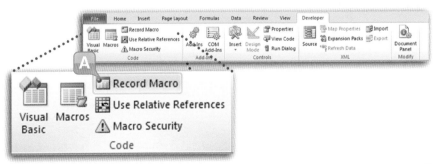

3. In the **Record Macro** dialog box:

- Provide a name for your macro in the **Macro name:** field. Create a descriptive name rather than something like "macro1."

- Identify a shortcut key (it must be a letter) for your macro in the **Shortcut key:** textbox. This is the key you press on your keyboard to run your macro after recording it.

- Choose a location where you want your macro to be stored from the **Store macro in:** dropdown 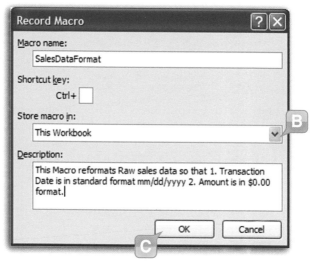.

- Provide a clear description of what your macro does in the **Description:** field so you (and others) can remember its purpose.

4. Click the **OK** button. If there are no problems with your macro information, recording begins immediately. If there are problems (such as if the shortcut key you selected was already in use), correct the problems and then press the **OK** button again.

5. Perform the actions you want to record in your macro. The actions recorded for the sample macro are listed here:

- Select **Column B**, then use the tools in the **Format Cells** dialog box (accessed from the **Number** group on the **Home** tab) to format the data as MM/DD/YYYY.

- Select **Column C**, then use the tools in the **Format Cells** dialog box to format the data as currency ($0.00).

6. Click the **Stop Recording** button  in the **Code** group on the **Developer** tab.

7. To run your macro, click the **Macros** button  in the **Code** group on the **Developer** tab to launch the **Macro** dialog box . Select the macro you want to use, then click the **Run** button.

 Bright Idea: Add a macro to your **Quick Access** toolbar. See the **Customize Quick Access Toolbar** tip for complete customization instructions. To access your list of macros during customization, select **Macros** from the **Choose commands from:** dropdown menu.

41 | Bookmark Cells and Groups of Cells for Easy Reference

Difficulty: ⬤⬤◯◯

PROBLEM You are working with a very large spreadsheet that handles expenses and reimbursements for on-the-road salespeople. You have a standard per-mile gasoline charge that then has a regional multiplier attached to it (to account for gas prices that are higher in some areas than others.) You would like an easy way to apply that multiplier to the relevant salespeople.

SOLUTION Create a named cell or named range. A named cell is a cell that, while still locatable by its coordinates, also carries a name that the user defines. Naming a range "Gas-Northeast," for example, would make it very easy to apply that multiplier to your spreadsheet by region.

A named range is a group of cells that you name. For example, if you have a sheet that covers twenty years, worth of data, you may have a series of analysis tables that isolate particular months and years. Somewhere, hundreds of rows down or columns across, is your collection of data covering quarterly reports for the year 2002. Naming a range "Q3_2002_Data" makes finding that specific information much easier.

> 💬 **What Microsoft Calls It:** Named Cells & Ranges

📑 Step-by-Step

Create a Named Range of Cells

1. Select the cells you want to name .

	BK	BL	BM	BN	BO
	3Q 2002 Target	**3Q 2002 Finals**	**3Q 2002 Returns**	**3Q 2002 Actuals**	**3Q Avg 1992-2002**
370					
371	$10,000.00	$ 9,763.00	$ (1,212.00)	$ 8,551.00	$ 9,893.00
372	$13,000.00	$14,558.00	$ (2,678.00)	$11,880.00	$ 12,506.00
373	$ 5,000.00	$ 8,954.00	$ (3,002.00)	$ 5,952.00	$ 4,429.00
374	$ 1,500.00	$22,669.00	$ (8,764.00)	$13,905.00	$ 1,235.00
375	$25,000.00	$37,884.00	$ (300.00)	$37,584.00	$ 225,523.00

2. Click the **Formulas** tab.

3. In the **Defined Names** group, click the **Define Name** button 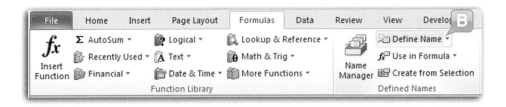.

4. Type a name for your range in the **Name:** textbox C. Note that names must begin with an underscore or letter and cannot contain spaces.

5. Select the scope of the range from the **Scope:** dropdown menu D. The scope defines where the name will be saved. You can apply it to a whole workbook (so that range name typed in any sheet in the workbook will bring you to that location) or you can confine it to a single sheet.

6. Click the **OK** button E.

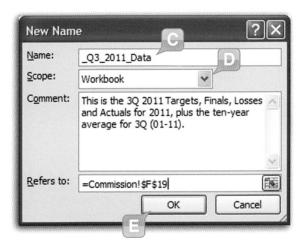

42 | Insert a Chart

Difficulty: ⦿⦿⦿◯

PROBLEM You want to illustrate which sales associates have contributed the most sales during a set period. A chart would convey that information better than raw data.

SOLUTION Insert a chart into your sheets. Charts provide an easy-to-assemble but clear and persuasive illustration of your data. Excel offers a variety of charts in both two-dimensional and three-dimensional formats.

See Also: Appendix B

	A	B	C	D	E
1	Item	Category	Store	Associate	Sale Price
2	Dishwasher	Appliance	1123	Andrews	$ 208.00
3	Stove	Appliance	1123	Cook	$ 623.00
4	Refrigerator	Appliance	1123	Flaherty	$ 650.00
5	Home Thtr	Audio	1123	Johnson	$ 821.00
6	Refrigerator	Appliance	1123	Andrews	$ 998.00
7	Stereo	Audio	1123	Cook	$ 395.00
8	Home Thtr	Audio	1123	Flaherty	$ 377.00
9	Home Thtr	Audio	1123	Johnson	$ 534.00
10	BluRay	Video	1123	Andrews	$ 399.00
11	Refrigerator	Appliance	1123	Cook	$ 873.00
12	Stereo	Audio	1123	Flaherty	$ 398.00
13	Dishwasher	Appliance	1123	Johnson	$ 559.00

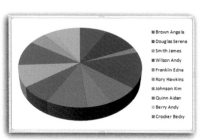

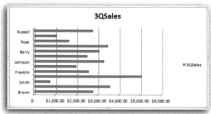

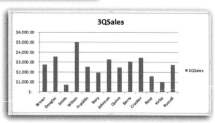

Step-by-Step

Use this method when you want more chart options or if you want to fine-tune the way the data appears.

1. Select the data you want to chart 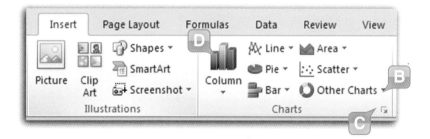. Make sure you highlight header rows and columns if you want the labels included on the chart.

	A	C	D	E
1	**Last Name**	**3Q Sales**	**mm %**	**Commission**
2	Brown	$ 2,751.00	6%	$ 165.06
3	Douglas	$ 3,552.00	4%	$ 142.08
4	Smith	$ 726.00	10%	$ 72.60
5	Wilson	$ 5,041.00	12%	$ 604.92
6	Franklin	$ 2,547.00	4%	$ 101.88
7	Rory	$ 1,961.00	6%	$ 117.66
8	Johnson	$ 3,275.00	6%	$ 196.50
9	Quinn	$ 2,486.00	4%	$ 99.44
10	Berry	$ 3,051.00	12%	$ 366.12
11	Crocker	$ 3,462.00	10%	$ 346.20
12	Rose	$ 1,618.00	6%	$ 97.08
13	Kirby	$ 1,042.00	6%	$ 62.52
14	Russell	$ 2,751.00	4%	$ 110.04

2. In the **Charts** group on the **Insert** tab, click the dropdown button for the chart type you want to use. To access charts not shown in the box, click the **Other Charts** button B, or click the **Charts** dialog box launcher C. **Column** D was selected for this example.

3. Select the specific chart from the dropdown menu panel that appears. **3D Pyramid** 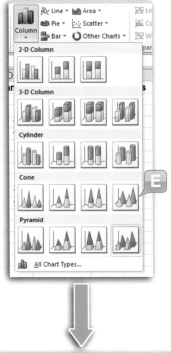 was selected for this example.

4. Review the chart, and make any changes you need to the design or layout.

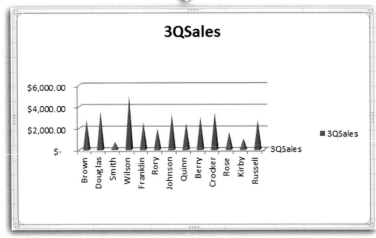

Quickest Click: Insert a Chart

Use this method when you want a quick visual snapshot of your data. Highlight the data you want to chart, then press the **F11** key on your keyboard. Excel chooses what it thinks is the best chart type for your data, and a basic chart is created on a new worksheet added to the left of the sheet that contained the data you charted.

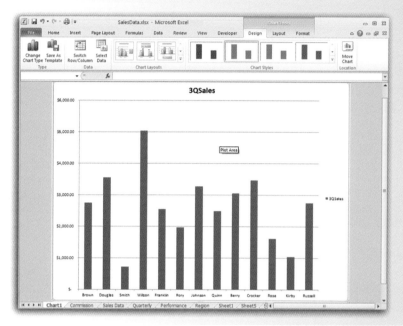

STOP

43 | Determine If Your Data Shows a Relevant Trend

Difficulty: ⬤⬤⬤◯

PROBLEM You have a workbook that contains a full twelve months of your factory's widget production. Even after graphing the data, it is just not clear if production went up or down over the course of the year.

SOLUTION Insert a trendline. With a trendline, you can see if your sales went up, and if so, by how much. Charts reveal a great deal about your data in a dynamic, accessible format. Sometimes, swings in the data make it difficult to discern if there is an important trend in the information. Trendlines perform calculations behind the scenes and provide an indicator of the direction your data is moving to help make the big picture clear.

Including a trendline in your charts may help illustrate both the size and direction of changes in your data. They are also useful in forecasting future or past values based on available data.

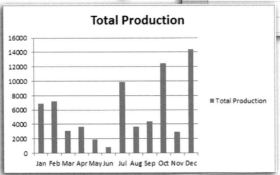

	A	B
1	**Month**	**Total Production**
2	Jan	6862.72
3	Feb	7217.9
4	Mar	3093.53
5	Apr	3676.7
6	May	1939
7	Jun	877.2
8	Jul	9867.22
9	Aug	3691.35
10	Sep	4408.08
11	Oct	12491.9
		2929.2
		14426.73

What Microsoft Calls It: Add a Trendline to Your Chart

 Step-by-Step

Add a Trendline to Your Chart

1. Right-click on any data bar in the chart and select **Add Trendline** from the menu that appears 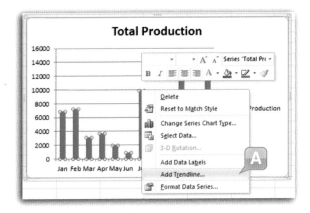.

2. For a basic trendline indicating the general direction of your data, click the radio button to the left of **Linear** B to select that option.

3. Click the **Display R-squared value on chart** checkbox C.

4. Click the **Close** button D.

 CONTINUE

5. Review your chart with the trendline in place 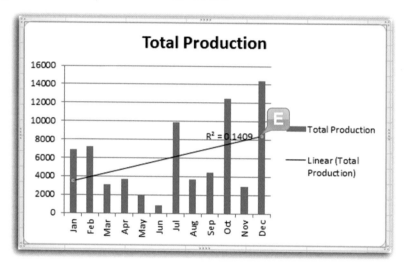. Note that the R-squared value on the trendline is 0.3429. In the simplest terms, this means that the downward trend the line indicates is roughly 34% accurate—meaning that while there is an apparent drop in production, it is not statistically significant. The closer a trend is to "1," or 100%, the more accurate it is. Most trends should not be considered significant until they are at least 0.5, or 50%.

Bright Idea: Excel 2010 offers a live preview option with this feature. Drag the **Format Trendline** dialog box off to the side and click through the various trendline options.The trendline's shape will change as your data is analyzed in different ways.

44 | Create a Chart from Your PivotTable

Difficulty: ⬤⬤⬤◯

PROBLEM You have data with thousands of donors and their annual gifts listed. The PivotTable you are using still doesn't help you see which donors gave the most or how many donors gave you donations at various giving tiers.

SOLUTION Create a PivotChart. You may need a visual representation of PivotTable information for a PowerPoint slide, a meeting agenda, a report, or faster analysis. A PivotChart gives you the snapshot of that data that you need.

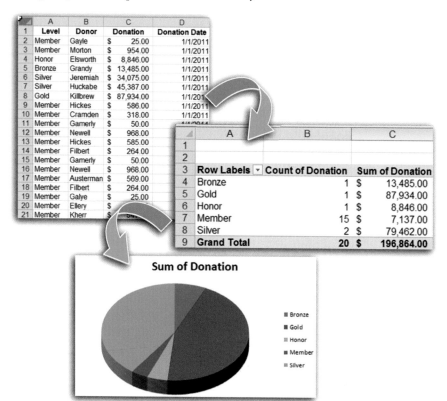

What Microsoft Calls It: Insert a PivotChart

Step-by-Step

Create a PivotChart

Option:
a.   Go directly from your data to a PivotChart (which creates a PivotTable in the process) by clicking a cell within the data you want to chart.
b.   Create a PivotChart from an existing PivotTable by clicking any field in the PivotTable to select it.

1. If you selected option **a.** from above, click the lower half of the **PivotTable** combo button **A** in the **Tables** group of the **Insert** tab and select **PivotChart** **B**.

   If you selected option **b.** from above, click the **PivotChart** button **C** in the **Tools** group of the **Options** tab in the highlighted **PivotTable Tools** section of the ribbon.

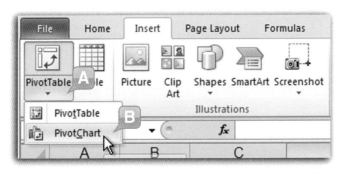

CONTINUE

2. If you chose option **a.**, Excel chooses the chart type it believes is most appropriate to your data.

   If you select option **b.**, the **Insert Chart** dialog box 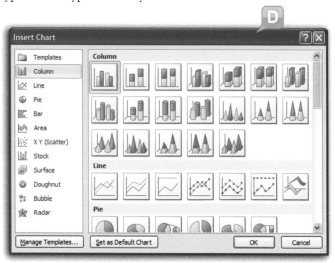 appears where you can select the type and subtype of chart you want to insert.

3. Review your chart 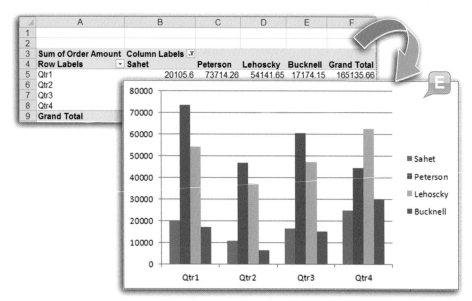.

Bright Idea: You can change the info displayed just like in a PivotTable. Drag and drop fields to change X axis, Y axis, filter, or the data displayed.

45 | Insert a SmartArt Graphic

Difficulty: ⬤◯◯◯

PROBLEM You need to explain that changes to one element of a project will impact development time, cost, customer response, and, therefore, revenue. You need a way to convey this complicated process and show the relevant relationships.

SOLUTION Use SmartArt graphics. Data can be compelling information, but often you need to express it graphically to help others understand what the numbers mean. Charts and process maps created with the powerful SmartArt tool provide visually appealing, dynamic images to convey information clearly.

SmartArt graphics are divided into seven categories. Some graphics can be used to express multiple concepts and so appear in more than one category. Here is a list of the categories and an explanation for each:

- **All**: This is not a category. By choosing this option, you can view all graphics from all categories.
- **List**: These graphics are best used to express static lists of information.
- **Process**: These graphics are best used to express processes and procedures where there are multiple steps with various effects, consequences, and paths.
- **Cycle**: These graphics are best used to express cyclical events or repetitive processes.
- **Hierarchy**: These graphics are best used to display groups or lists where one item takes precedence over another.
- **Relationship**: These graphics are best used to display information that is connected to or dependent on other information, resources, or processes.
- **Matrix**: These graphics are best used to show the relationship of information or components to a whole.
- **Pyramid**: These graphics combine hierarchy and relationship. Higher levels depend on the items in the levels opposite.

Step-by-Step

1. Click the **SmartArt** button 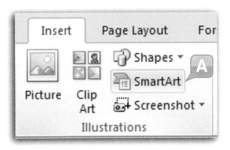 in the **Illustrations** group of the **Insert** tab.

2. In the **Choose a SmartArt Graphic** dialog box, select a **SmartArt** category from the left panel **B** to reveal the graphic options for that category in the center panel **C**.

3. Click a graphic **D** to reveal a sample of what it will look like once it is inserted in the right panel **E**. This panel also includes a brief description of the graphic and the information it would best be used to convey.

4. When you have found the graphic you want to insert, make sure it is selected and then click the **OK** button **F**.

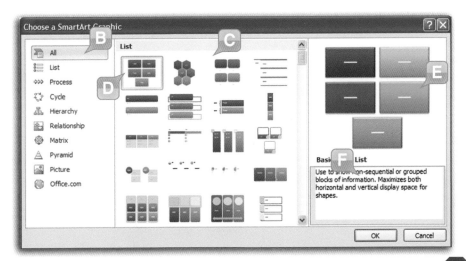

STOP

46 Configure a SmartArt Graphic

Difficulty: ⬤◯◯◯

PROBLEM You have prepared a report using SmartArt graphics that conveys the information clearly, but you also want it to appeal visually to your audience. You would like to use your company's colors and design a crisp, professional look.

SOLUTION Use the SmartArt design panel to implement the look and feel you want. When you insert or select a SmartArt graphic, two new tabs appear: the Smart Art Tools Design tab and the Smart Art Tools Format tab. The Design tab options let you make color and layout selections for the graphic as a whole, while the Format tab lets you drill down and make choices about the individual shape and WordArt elements in the graphic.

Step-by-Step

Configure a SmartArt Graphic

1. Select the graphic so it is active. You can tell a graphic is selected or active if you can see the border around the items **A**.

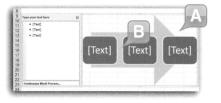

2. Select an area marked **[Text] B**, and begin typing to enter your information into the graphic **C**.

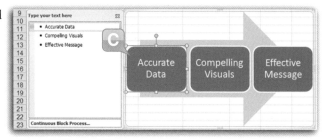

3. Once you have entered all of your text elements, use the tools on the **SmartArt Tools Design** and **SmartArt Tools Format** tabs to adjust the appearance of your graphic.

Design Tab:

- **Create Graphic Group**: Here you can insert additional items (the **Add Bullet** button), elements (the **Add Shape** button), or adjust the direction of the graphic.

- **Layouts Group**: In this section you can adjust the entire graphic.

- **SmartArt Styles Group**: These tools let you change the look and feel of your graphic (borders, drop shadows, rotation, reflection etc.).

- **Reset**: This button returns the graphic to its original state before you started making adjustments.

Format Tab:

- **Shapes**: These tools let you select an element or group of elements in your graphic and change their shape. In the example at right, you could change the rounded squares containing text to circles.

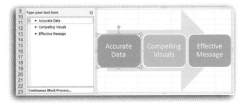

- **Shape Styles**: Here you can adjust the look and feel of an element or group of elements. In the example at right, you could change the rounded squares from a white outline with blue fill to a blue outline with a white fill and a shadow.

- **WordArt Styles**: Most SmartArt graphic text is displayed in WordArt. As a result, you can change the appearance of the text with many settings, including color, outline, shadow, 3D, and more.

- **Arrange**: This button gives you access to change the arrangement of the elements within your SmartArt graphic, and the arrangement of multiple graphics on the page (if you have more than one).

- **Size**: This button gives you access to tools that will allow you to change the physical (print) size of the SmartArt graphic.

47

Select and Apply a Theme to Your Documents

Difficulty: ⬤◯◯◯

PROBLEM You have created a collection of documents—a PowerPoint presentation, a Word meeting agenda, and your new Excel spreadsheet with charts—and you want them all to share the same look and feel.

SOLUTION Apply a Theme. **Document Themes** are sets of colors, fonts, and other formatting details that, together, give your document collection a cohesive identity. When documents have a unified and polished appearance, they make a more professional, positive impression.

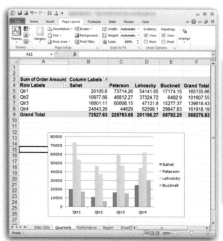

Autumn Theme in Excel

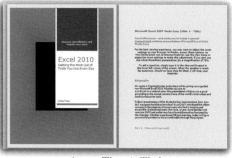

Autumn Theme in Word

What Microsoft Calls It: Document Themes or Themes

 Step-by-Step

Select and Apply a Document Theme

1. Click the **Themes** button in the **Themes** panel of the **Page Layout** tab.

2. Hover over themes in the **Built In** selection panel **B** to preview the theme on your worksheet. Note: Unless you have a visible chart/graph or SmartArt item, some changes to cells with background fills, colored text, or style sets may be confined to font selection and therefore will be hard to see.

Options: If you have an active internet connection, you may choose from even more themes under the **From Office.com** section of the **Themes** combo box **C**.

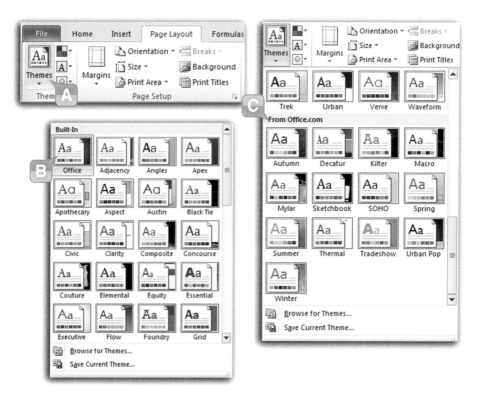

4. When you have found the theme that suits your needs, just click to apply.

5. Examine your results  D E F, and, if applicable, review your associated documents (such as an agenda in Word or your presentation in PowerPoint) to be sure you like the look there as well.

6. Save your worksheet with the changes.

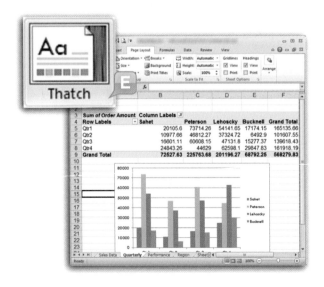

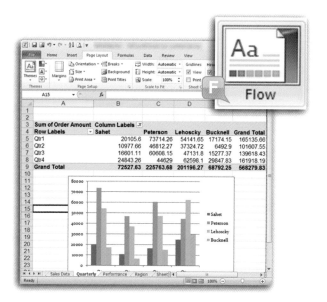

48 | Make Your Own Theme

Difficulty: ◉◉◉◯

PROBLEM You are working on a new marketing effort that requires particular design elements and a specific look and feel. These elements include specific color combinations to match your corporate logo and so on. The built-in document themes are not sufficient to meet your design needs.

SOLUTION Create a custom Theme.

> **What Microsoft Calls It:** Customize Document Themes

Step-by-Step

Customizing a Theme

1. Apply the theme that best matches your needs to your document.

2. Make your adjustments to color, font, and design elements using the tools available on the **Ribbon**:

   • On the **Home** tab in the **Styles** and **Cells** group.

   • On the **Insert** tab in the **Text** group.

   • On the **Page Layout** tab in the **Themes** group.

3. Click the **Themes** button in the **Themes** group of the **Page Layout** tab.

4. Click the **Save Current Theme** option at the bottom of the **Built-In** theme selection panel.

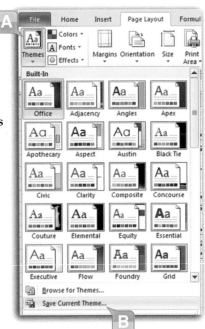

5. Enter a name for your theme in the **File name:** textbox .

6. Click the **Save** button D.

 Hot Tip: You'll notice when you save your theme that the file type (in the **Save as Type:** textbox E) is **Office Theme(*.thmx)**. This means that your new theme will be available in other Office applications. You may need to make additions or small changes when you use a theme created in another application, but your custom theme will be ready to use for most projects.

STOP

49 | Add Information to the Tops or Bottoms of Printed Pages

Difficulty: ⬤◯◯◯

PROBLEM You produce identical reports on a regular basis, reflecting the most current data. You need a way to keep track of the report versions at a glance.

SOLUTION Insert a Header and Footer. Headers and footers provide an excellent means of tracking version data, including revision dates and author changes. They can also make deciphering report information easier through the inclusion of navigation aids like page numbers, footnotes, and legends.

 What Microsoft Calls It: Insert a Header and Footer

Step-by-Step

Insert and Configure Headers and Footers

1. Click the **Header & Footer** button **A** in the **Text** group of the **Insert** tab. This converts your workbook to page layout view and launches the **Header & Footer Tools Design** tab **B**.

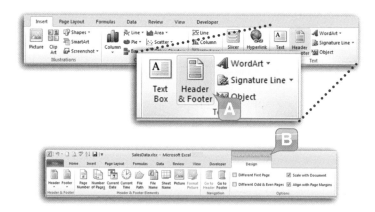

2. Set up your header and footer using the tools in the **Design** tab groups.

- **Header & Footer** group C: Click one of these buttons to select pre-set header and footer formatting options.
- **Header & Footer Elements** group D: Insert and configure only the elements you want, one at a time.
  - » **Page Number**: Displays the page number.
  - » **Number of Pages**: Displays the total number of pages in the sheet.
  - » **Current Date**: Displays the current date each time the sheet is opened.
  - » **Current Time**: Displays the current time when the sheet is opened.
  - » **File Path**: Displays the full path to the file's location, including network locations.
  - » **File Name**: Displays the full file name.
  - » **Sheet Name**: Displays the name of the individual sheet.
  - » **Picture**: Inserts a picture.
  - » **Format Picture**: Becomes active if you have a picture inserted and selected, and allows you configure the image.

- **Navigation** group E: Move between the header and footer.
- **Options** group F: Select how and on which pages headers and footers appear and how they will print.

 Caution: Each worksheet has its own header, so make sure the worksheet to which you want to apply a header is active.

50 | Page Setup

Difficulty: ⬤◯◯◯

PROBLEM You are happy with a spreadsheet. It displays the data you need onscreen and looks great. When you go to print, however, the result on paper is not as appealing as you'd like.

SOLUTION Configure your print page using the Print Preview window and the Page Setup dialog box.

Configuring your print page can be confusing, but Microsoft has provided tools to make this configuration relatively easy—once you know what they are and how to use them. Making adjustments on the Print Preview screen is the fastest method for preparing a sheet to print. The arguably better way is to adjust those settings before you get there. By setting up your sheet to consistently print in a particular way with particular settings, you save time and effort for yourself and your colleagues who may also need to print the sheet. 💡

Step-by-Step

Page Setup Using the Page Setup Dialog Box Options

1. Launch the **Page Setup** dialog box using either the **Page Setup** dialog box launcher  in the **Page Setup** group of the **Page Layout** tab or the **Page Setup** link **B** on the **Print** Backstage View under the **File** tab.

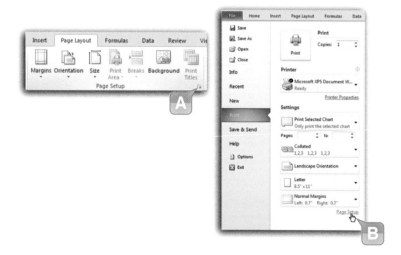

2. Make your formatting selections on the **Page**, **Margins**, **Header/Footer** and **Sheet** tabs.

- **Page** : The options on this tab allow you to set basic page layout and printing preferences.
- **Margins** **D**: Here you can set page margins and header and footer size measurements.

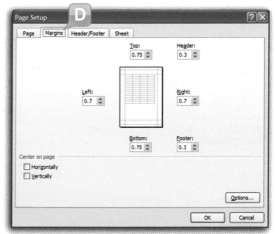

- **Header/Footer** 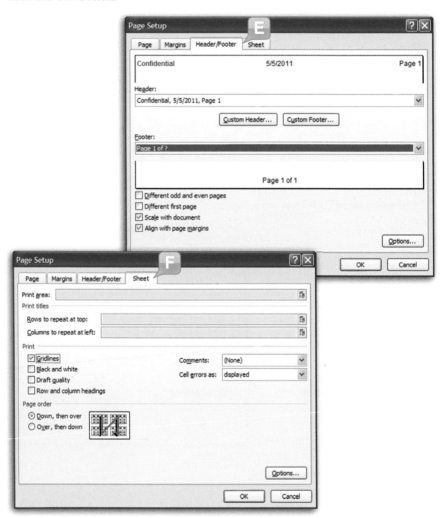: On this tab you can create a header and/or footer. You can also determine the Header and Footer dimensions and the pages on which they occur.

- **Sheet** : These selections allow you to define the print area, select rows and/ or columns to be repeated on each page, select items to be printed or hidden, and determine page print order for worksheets that take up two or more pages vertically and horizontally.

3. Click the **OK** button.

Quickest Clicks: Some of the most common layout options are available to right on the **Ribbon** in the **Page Setup** panel 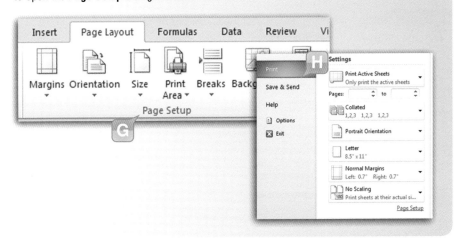 on the **Page Layout** tab and in the **Print** Backstage View under the **File** tab. Access settings such as simple **Margins, Orientation, Size, Print Area, Page Breaks** and **Print Titles** quickly without having to open the **Page Setup** dialog box first.

Hot Tip: Use the **Page Layout** view as you are creating and editing your worksheets to see how your document will appear when printed. Access the page layout view by clicking on the **Page Layout** button 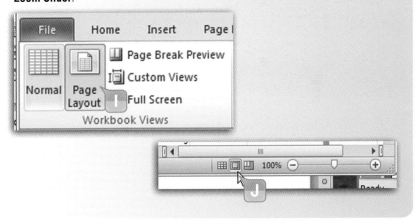 in the **Workbook Views** on the **View** tab, or by clicking on the **Page Layout** button on the status bar, to the left of the **Zoom Slider**.

51 | Choose Which Part of Your Worksheet to Print

Difficulty:

PROBLEM You have a large worksheet that contains more data than you need for a report you want to print out and take to a meeting.

SOLUTION Print only the portion you want or need by setting a print area, or clearing a print area. Clear the print area between each new print job.

> **What Microsoft Calls It:** Setting a print area, Clearing a print area

Step-by-Step

Using the Page Setup Dialog Box to Set a Print Area

1. Click the **Page Setup** dialog box launcher .

2. Click the **Sheet** tab 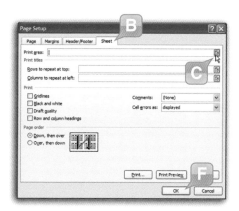.

3. Click the **Print Area:** action button C.

4. Click and drag on your worksheet to select the area you want to print.

5. The selected area will be displayed as absolute cell references in the **Page Setup Print area:** dialog box D and will be surrounded by a dotted line E.

6. When finished, press the **ENTER** key on your keyboard.

7. Click the **OK** button F.

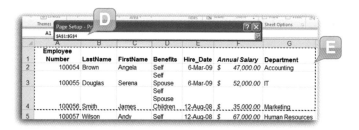

Bright Idea: Select non-adjacent columns and rows for printing by holding the **CTRL** key on your keyboard while you select them. Note that each segment of non-adjacent data prints on its own page.

Quickest Click: Use the **Print Area** Button to Define a Print Area.
First, highlight the cells you want to print **G**. Then, click the **Print Area** button in the **Page Setup** group of the **Page Layout** tab and select **Set Print Area** **H**.

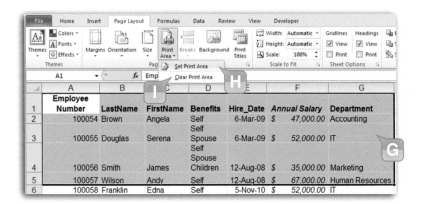

Quickest Click: Clearing a Print Area.
Click the **Print Area** button in the **Page Setup** group of the **Page Layout** tab and select **Clear Print Area** .

52 | Print Multiple Worksheets

Difficulty: ⬤◯◯◯

PROBLEM You have a workbook that contains multiple worksheets and you need to print all the relevant sheets, including related PivotTables and charts.

SOLUTION Print the worksheets individually (if you need to make special print selections on each one), or use the CTRL key to select multiple sheets and print all at once.

See Also: Choose Which Part of Your Worksheet to Print; Page Setup; Print to a Specific Number of Pages

Step-by-Step

Printing Multiple Worksheets

1. Press and hold the **CTRL** key on your keyboard while you click the tabs for the worksheets you want to print Ⓐ Ⓑ Ⓒ.

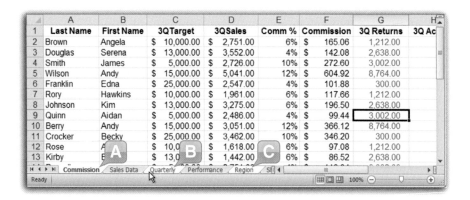

2. Click the **File** tab, then click the **Print** to view the **Print Preview** pane **E**. Confirm that the appropriate pages will print. Note that each worksheet will print on its own pages(s).

3. Click the **Print** button **F**.

Bright Idea: You may also choose to print multiple workbooks at once. To do so, click the **File** tab and choose **Open**. Select multiple documents by holding the **SHIFT** key (for adjacent documents) or **CTRL** key (for non-adjacent documents) on your keyboard while you make your selections, then click the **Tools** button and select **Print**.

53 | Print to a Specific Number of Pages

Difficulty: ●○○○

PROBLEM You have a worksheet that you want to print and hand out at a meeting. When you do, though, you find that the sheet stretches across multiple horizontal pages, making it difficult to review.

SOLUTION Excel has several tools to help you layout your sheet onto the number of pages you want to print in a visually clear alignment.

The first thing to do is make sure that your page is set up for **Landscape** rather than **Portrait** page orientation. You can quickly adjust this by clicking the **Orientation** button Ⓐ in the **Page Setup** group of the **Page Layout** tab and then clicking the **Landscape** option Ⓑ.

See Also: Choose Which Part of Your Worksheet to Print; Page Setup; Print Multiple Worksheets

Next, determine where your page breaks are. There are two ways to do this:

- Set your print area. Page breaks are identified with a dashed line Ⓒ.

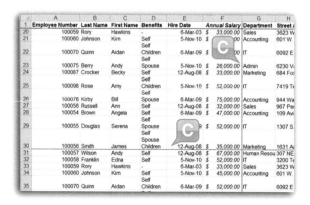

- Click the **Page Break Preview** button 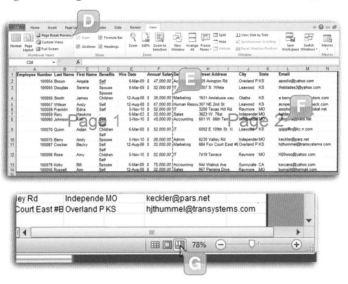 in the **Workbook Views** group of the **View** tab. This reveals the current page breaks (thick blue dashed lines) and the page numbers. You can also quickly get to **Page Break Preview** by clicking on the **Page Break Preview** button in the status bar.

Once you determine that the data does extend beyond a single page, adjust print settings to force the worksheet onto a single page by clicking and dragging the break lines with your mouse.

Step-by-Step

Print to a Specific Number of Pages

1. Click the **Page Setup** dialog box launcher  on the **Page Layout** tab.

2. Click the **Fit to:** radio button **J**.

3. Adjust the **pages wide by pages tall** numbers in the controls **K** **L**.

4. Click the **OK** button **M**.

5. Use the **Print Preview** or **Page Break Preview** functions to verify the page breaks appear where you want them to.

Quickest Click: Print to a Specific Number of Pages

While in **Page Break Preview**, click the **Scale:** reduce button (thus reducing the scale from 100% where you started, which is full-sized) until the page break indicator has merged with the page border (the thick blue solid line) and includes all of the data to the right of the break . Use the print preview to see how small (and potentially illegible) the adjustment made before you print.

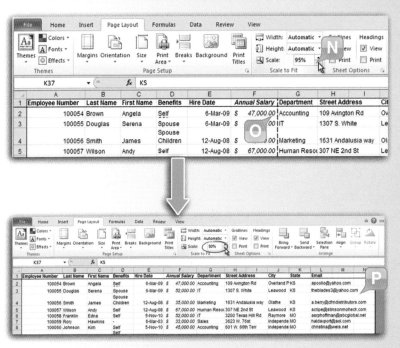

54 | Link Worksheets Together

Difficulty: ⬤⬤⬤◯

PROBLEM In your charity organization, one volunteer prepares a sheet with donation information that is used by several departments. One department tracks gifts for sending out thank-you notes, another creates press releases, and a third does analysis for case studies and fundraising. Rather than having each of those departments re-enter the data individually, you want a way for the related sheets to share the necessary information.

SOLUTION Link the worksheets. Worksheets can be linked so that information shared between the two is always identical. This reduces errors and ensures consistency, as information only needs to be entered in one place to be available in multiple locations.

> **What Microsoft Calls It:** External Reference Links

Step-by-Step

Link Worksheets

1. Open both the source and destination (dependent) **B** workbooks.

2. In the dependent workbook, select a cell **C** where you want to place the formula that will link that cell to the source data.

3. Enter the formula up to the point where you would refer to the source cell 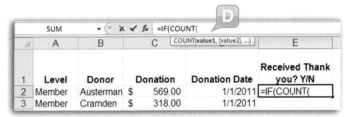.

In this example, you now need to see if the donor has received a thank you note by referencing the *Thank You Card Date* in the *Donor Thank You* workbook. The COUNT function will return a value of "1" (if a date has been entered) or a "0" if a date has not been entered.

4. Switch to the source workbook and select the cell E or data range you need for the formula in the dependent workbook. Excel recognizes you are creating a link and displays the formula in the formula bar F.

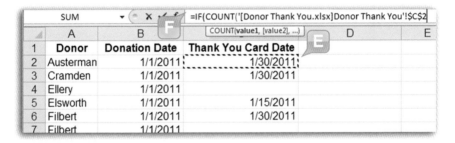

5. Return to the destination workbook and complete the formula G.

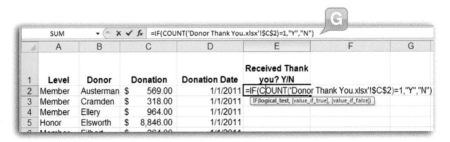

CONTINUE

6. Press the **Enter** key on your keyboard to see the cell populated 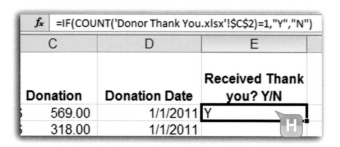. In this example a "Y" should appear if the donor has received a card, and an "N" if they have not.

	f_x	=IF(COUNT('Donor Thank You.xlsx'!C2)=1,"Y","N")	
	C	D	E
	Donation	**Donation Date**	**Received Thank you? Y/N**
	569.00	1/1/2011	Y
	318.00	1/1/2011	

7. Repeat as necessary to complete your links.

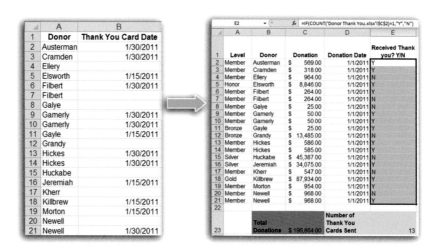

Note that any cells dependent upon your linked cell will also compute and populate .

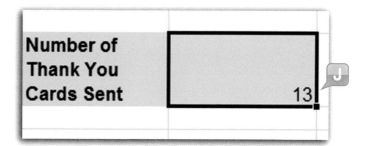

Bright Idea: If you plan to apply your links to an entire column of data, change the references from absolute to relative and simply fill down the column.

55

Prepare Your Spreadsheet Data for Use in Access

Difficulty: ⬤⬤⬤◯

PROBLEM The information you have been analyzing and tracking with Excel workbooks has outgrown Excel's size limitations. Because you would also like to expand the use of the information, and add and maintain multiple relationships between disparate pieces of information, you decide that your data should be incorporated into a larger and more comprehensive Access data store. You do not want to re-enter all your existing data from scratch in your new Access database.

SOLUTION Prepare your Excel data for export. ⚠

 **Step-by-Step**

Prepare Data for Export to Acces

1. Adjust your column headers so they contain no spaces or punctuation (underscores can be used to replace spaces, but all other punctuation marks should be removed).

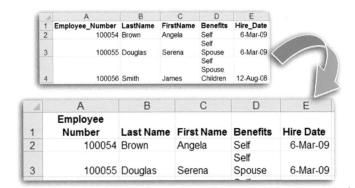

2. If you are exporting your data for import to a database that contains the same or similar information, make sure your column headers match the corresponding ones from the database and that you have the same number of columns as the database for which the information is being prepared.

3. Make sure your worksheet is formatted as a table.
   - Select the data you want to define as a table, including column headers 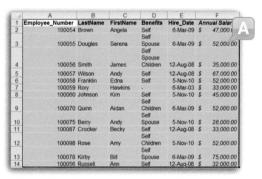.

   - Click the **Table** button 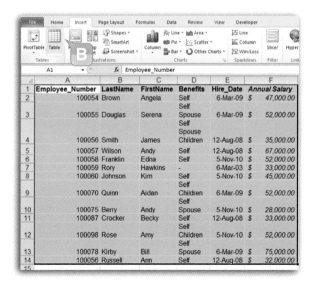 in the **Tables** group of the **Insert** tab to launch the **Create Table** dialog box.

- Check the **My table has headers** checkbox .
- Click the **OK** button.

4. Eliminate any blank columns, rows, and cells within the data to be exported. You may either eliminate the record containing the empty cells, or you can insert a placeholder value (such as a 0 or NULL). Blank columns and rows at the "ends" of the sheet will be ignored.

Caution: You need to keep the capabilities of each program in mind before you move data between the two, and you need to consider the nature of the data before you move it. For example, Access allows a number of links between various data tables. These links are not necessarily supported or easily demonstrable when you move the information to Excel. You may need to remove duplicate information or split your data into multiple sheets to create the most effective export.

STOP

56 | Pull Data from a Website or Network Location

Difficulty: ◑◑◑◯

PROBLEM You have an old data system that was retired several years ago. The data from it was exported to a series of large, ungainly files. These files are kept on a shared drive on your company network and are too large to copy onto your local machine. You need to get to the information so you can query the historical sales data it includes without re-entering all the data.

SOLUTION Query your external data source directly from Excel. Sometimes the data you want or need is close at hand—an exported CSV file or even another Excel workbook from which you can import data. Other times, though, the data may be a bit more remote. Knowing how to connect to external data will save you a good deal of time over printing and re-entering it.

> **What Microsoft Calls It:** Query an External Data Source

Step-by-Step

Query an External Data Source

In this example, GNP data will be retrieved from the World Bank's public website.

1. Open a new worksheet.

2. Click the **From Web** button  in the **Get External Data** group of the **Data** tab.

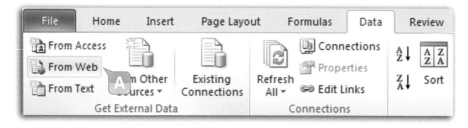

3. A special **New Web Query** browser window will open. Type the URL of the page from which you want to retrieve data in the address bar 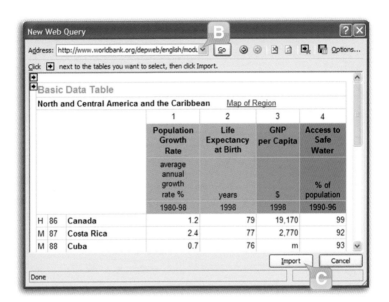 and press the ENTER key on your keyboard.

4. Click the yellow-boxed arrow associated with the data you want to import .
    The yellow box will turn green when you hover over it with your mouse, and then
    convert to a checkmark after you have clicked it.

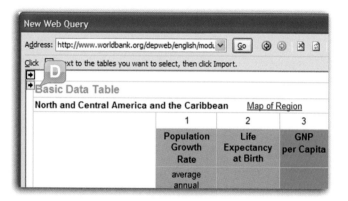

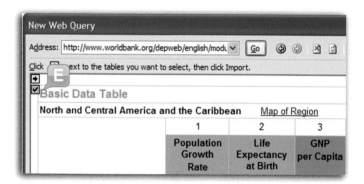

5. Click the **Import** button .

6. In the **Import Data** dialog box, select the **Existing Worksheet** radio button
    (since you created a new one just for this data back in Step 1).

7. Select the cell where the imported data will start its fill. The data will fill to the
    right and down as far as it needs to go to import all of it. In this example, the fill
    was started at cell F5.

8. Click the **OK** button.

9. Review your imported data 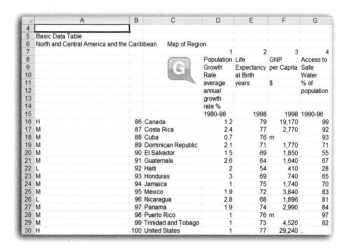.

	A	B	C	D	E	F	G
4							
5	Basic Data Table						
6	North and Central America and the Caribbean		Map of Region				
7				1	2	3	4
8				Population	Life	GNP	Access to
9				Growth	Expectancy	per Capita	Safe
10				Rate	at Birth		Water
11				average	years	$	% of
12				annual			population
13				growth			
14				rate %			
15				1980-98		1998	1998 1990-96
16	H		86 Canada	1.2	79	19,170	99
17	M		87 Costa Rica	2.4	77	2,770	92
18	M		88 Cuba	0.7	76 m		93
19	M		89 Dominican Republic	2.1	71	1,770	71
20	M		90 El Salvador	1.5	69	1,850	55
21	M		91 Guatemala	2.6	64	1,640	67
22	L		92 Haiti	2	54	410	28
23	M		93 Honduras	3	69	740	65
24	M		94 Jamaica	1	75	1,740	70
25	M		95 Mexico	1.9	72	3,840	83
26	L		96 Nicaragua	2.8	68	1,896	81
27	M		97 Panama	1.9	74	2,990	84
28	M		98 Puerto Rico	1	76 m		97
29	M		99 Trinidad and Tobago	1	73	4,520	82
30	H		100 United States	1	77	29,240	

STOP

57 | Personalize and Customize Documents

Difficulty: ◯◯◯◯

PROBLEM You are getting ready to send out a letter inviting people to your yearly donor appreciation banquet. You want to personalize each invitation with the donor's name and donation amount without typing in every name and address into your form letter.

SOLUTION Use Mail Merge to create your letters, envelopes, and RSVP cards.

Mail Merge is a tool in Microsoft Word that allows you to merge a list of data stored in a data source (an Excel spreadsheet, an Access database, a comma-separated value text file, etc.) with fields in a document.

There are several benefits to using a mail merge to create your documents.

- The process can save you a great deal of time and effort.
- Data can be stored one place and sent to you in a single ready-to-use file.
- Errors are reduced, as you are not retyping information already entered.
- Personalized communication tends to yield better results than form letters. 💡

> ### What Microsoft Calls It: Mail Merge

Step-by-Step

Create a Mail Merge with a Microsoft Word Document

1. Configure the Excel spreadsheet so that all data to be used in the merge is in columns.

2. Make sure that each column header contains only alphanumeric characters. Words may be separated by an underscore , but no other punctuation characters should be used.

	A	B	C	D	E
1	Donor_Level	Honorific	Donor	Donation	Donation Date
2	Bronze	Mrs.	Gayle	$ 25.00	1/1/2011
3	Member	Mr.	Morton	$ 954.00	1/1/2011
4	Honor	Dr. and Mrs.	Elsworth	$ 8,846.00	1/1/2011
5	Bronze	Professor	Grandy	$ 13,485.00	1/1/2011
6	Silver	Ms.	Jeremiah	$ 34,075.00	1/1/2011
7	Silver	Mr. and Dr.	Huckabe	$ 45,387.00	1/1/2011
8	Gold	Mr. and Mrs.	Killbrew	$ 87,934.00	1/1/2011

3. Save the workbook.

4. In Microsoft Word, prepare the document into which you intend to insert the merge data.

5. Click the **Start Mail Merge** dropdown button  in the **Start Mail Merge** group of the **Mailings** tab.

6. Select **Step by Step Mail Merge Wizard**.

7. Follow the steps of the **Mail Merge** wizard.

8. In Step 3 of the wizard (MS Word 2010), identify the worksheet you just created as your data source by clicking the **Browse** option under the **Use an existing list** heading.

9. Browse to the workbook you wish to use and click **Open**. The **Select Table** dialog box will pop up.

10. Select the sheet within the workbook where your data is located and click **OK**.

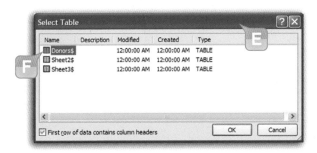

CONTINUE

11. The **Mail Merge Recipients**  dialog box will open. From this window, you can sort data by columns and filter, add, or remove recipients from your merge. When your recipients list is ready, click **OK**.

12. In Step 4, position your cursor where you would like to insert a merge field.

13. Click the **More Items** option  in the **Mail Merge** panel.

14. Select the field you want to insert  in the **Fields:** window.

15. Click the **Insert** button .

16. Repeat steps 12 through 15 as often as necessary to insert all required merge fields .

Your status as a «Donor_Level» Donor entitles you to 4 Tickets to the event and complimentary valet parking.

Dear «Honorific»«Donor»

In recognition of your generous contributions to our organization in the fiscal year 2009-2010, would love to invite you as a guest of honor to the 2011 Annual Appreciation Banquet.

17. Click the **Next: Preview your letters** link 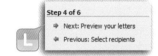.

18. Review the data in the merge fields .

Dear «Honorific» «Donor»

In recognition of your generous contributions to our would love to invite you as a guest of honor to the 2

Dear Mrs. Gayle

In recognition of your generous co
would love to invite you as a guest

Your status as a «Donor_Level» Donor entitles you to 4 Tickets to the event and complimentary valet parking.

Your status as a Bronze Donor entitle
to 4 Tickets to the event and complime

19. Click the **Next: Complete the merge link** 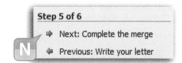.

Bright Idea: Use Mail Merge to populate fields in documents besides letters. The name "mail merge" is somewhat misleading, as the functionality is not limited to mail or even to correspondence. The merged data can be addresses for envelopes and labels, contact and personalization information for letters and emails, product information for flyers and catalogs, honoree information for certificates and diplomas—the possibilities are virtually endless.

STOP

58 | Sending Documents from Excel

Difficulty:

PROBLEM You regularly create workbooks that you distribute to your department via email attachments. You would like a faster way to do this this once each one is completed and save steps in clicking through file folders each time you attach the file.

SOLUTION Use the options in the **Save & Send** tab of the Backstage view to email workbooks directly from Excel. *Note: This tip only applies if you use Microsoft Outlook as your default e-mail client.*

Step-by-Step

Send Using E-mail

1. Click on the **File** tab, then click on the **Save & Send** tab **A** in the **Backstage View**. Make sure the **Send Using E-mail** sub-tab **B** is selected.

2. Choose how you want your workbook to be distributed by making a selection in the **Send Using E-mail** menu **C**.

- **Send as Attachment:** A copy of your workbook in its original file format 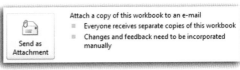 will be attached to an e-mail message.

  If there are multiple recipients, each will receive a separate copy. Changes made in these copies will not be reflected in the original or in the other copies. You will have to manually consolidate any changes and feedback from recipients into your original.

- **Send a Link:** An e-mail message will be opened that contains a URL link to the workbook .

  NOTE: This is only available if the workbook is saved in a shared location such as Windows Live SkyDrive. You will receive a warning 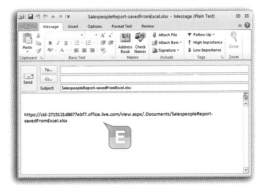 that this option will be unavailable if your workbook is not saved to a shared location.

  Sharing a workbook allows all recipients to edit the same copy of the document and view the most recent changes. You may also want to use this option if your worksheet is very large or you need to keep e-mail size small.

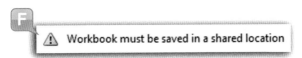

Workbook must be saved in a shared location

CONTINUE

- **Send as PDF:** A copy of your workbook will be converted to PDF format 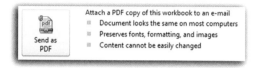 and attached to an e-mail message.

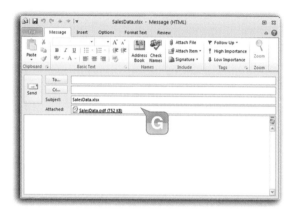

PDF format is useful because it looks the same on most computers, allowing you to control exactly what the recipient will see and print, including fonts, formatting and images. Recipients will not be able to change your original data, but they will be able to view your workbook, even if they do not have Excel installed on their machine. *Note: Your recipients will have to have a PDF reader installed on their computers to view the document. Readers such as Adobe's® Acrobat® Reader® are free and easily available.* ⚠

- **Send as XPS:** A copy of your workbook will be converted to XPS format  and attached to an e-mail message.

The XPS format offers many of the same benefits as PDF in addition to embedded fonts and more precise image and color rendering.

> **Caution:** When you click **Send as PDF**, the default **Save As PDF (*.pdf)** setting will be used. ALL worksheets and any **Page Setup** and **Print Area** adjustments you have made will be published into the PDF. Make sure you are satisfied with the results before you send your e-mail. If you don't like the way the PDF looks, make changes in **Page Setup** and review in the **Print Preview** panel before clicking **Send as PDF** again.

See Also: Page Setup; Choose Which Part of Your Worksheet to Print; and Print to a Specific Number of Pages

If you wish to e-mail a PDF or XPS of only certain worksheets within the workbook (or change other settings), click the **Create PDF/XPS Document** tab on the **Save & Send** panel. Click **Create PDF/XPS**  to open the **Publish as PDF or XPS** dialog box. Select **PDF (*.pdf)** in the **Save as type:** dropdown 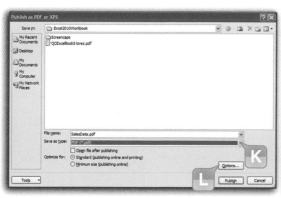, then click the **Options**  button to launch the **Options** dialog box and choose the settings you want for your PDF.

See Also: Choose a File Format When Saving a Workbook

59 Save Your Workbook to Windows Live SkyDrive

Difficulty: ⚪⚪⚪⚪

PROBLEM You frequently use several different computers—your desktop in the office, your laptop at home, and client workstations when you are traveling. You would like an easier way to update and view your workbooks without having to constantly copy them to thumb drives or email them from one machine to another.

SOLUTION Save your workbooks to Windows Live SkyDrive. With a Windows Live account, your SkyDrive acts as an external file folder that you can access via any machine with internet access. Changes you make will be available on any computer the next time you log in and work on the workbook.

Step-by-Step

Save your workbook to Windows Live SkyDrive

1. When your workbook is ready to share, go to the File tab, then click on the **Save & Send** tab  in the **Backstage View**.

2. Click **Save to Web** sub-tab B in the **Save & Send** pane.

3. If you have a Windows Live ID (or Hotmail, Messenger, or XBOX Live ID), click the **Sign In** button C.

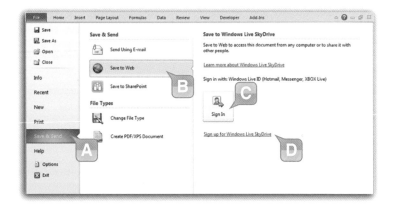

Hot Tip: If you need to create an ID, click **Sign up for Windows Live SkyDrive** D. Your default Web browser will launch to the Windows live login site. Click the **Sign up** button E and follow the directions to create an account.

4. Enter your account's e-mail address in the **E-mail address:** text box F and your Windows Live password in the **Password:** text box G in the **Connecting to docs.live.net** dialog box. Click **OK**.

5. In the **Backstage View**, your **Save to Windows Live SkyDrive** pane will change to show your account name H and SkyDrive folders I. Click on the **Save As** button J.

6. In the **Save As** dialog box, type in the name you want to give your workbook in the **File name:** text box . Click the **Save** button. Your document is now saved on your Windows Live SkyDrive.

Step-by-Step

Opening a document from SkyDrive

1. When you are ready to open a workbook from your SkyDrive, go to the **File** tab, then click on the **Save & Send** tab Ⓐ in the Backstage view.

2. Click **Save to Web** sub-tab Ⓑ in the **Save & Send** pane.

3. Click the **Sign In** button and log in to Windows Live.

4. When your **Save to Windows Live SkyDrive** pane has updated to show your account name Ⓗ and SkyDrive folders Ⓘ, click on the **Open** tab Ⓛ in the **File** menu.

5. In the **Open** dialog box click on the **My Network Places** button . Now that you are logged in to Windows Live, you will see your SkyDrive folders under the **My Network Places** dropdown. Double click the SkyDrive folder that contains your workbook , then select the workbook you wish to open .

6. Click the **Open** button .

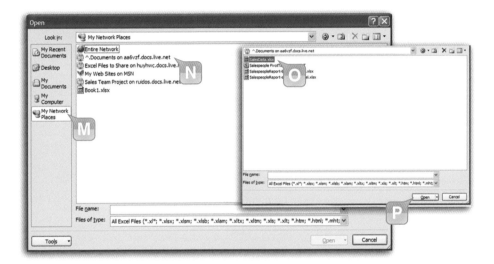

60 | Create a New Folder on Windows Live SkyDrive

Difficulty: ◖◖◖◯

PROBLEM You have several workbooks that you keep on your SkyDrive for easy access from different computers. You would like to organize your files by project so you can find them more quickly and keep track of versions more easily.

SOLUTION Create folders and sub-folders to organize your files.

Just like on your local hard drive, you can create folders and sub-folders on your Windows Live SkyDrive. Since all files and folders are accessed through a Web browser, it is somewhat more difficult to create and organize folders on your SkyDrive. Once you become comfortable with the SkyDrive user interface, however, you will be able to organize your files for quick reference and sharing.

 Step-by-Step

Create a new folder on your SkyDrive from Excel

1. When you are ready to open a workbook from your SkyDrive, go to the **File** tab, then click on the **Save & Send** tab **A** in the Backstage view.

2. Click **Save to Web** sub-tab **B** in the **Save & Send** pane.

3. Click the **Sign In** button **C** and log in to Windows Live.

4. When your **Save to Windows Live SkyDrive** pane has updated to show your account name  and SkyDrive folders, click on the **Windows Live SkyDrive** link above the **Personal Folders** heading. This will launch your default Web browser and open a window to your Windows Live folders.

5. In the **New** dropdown 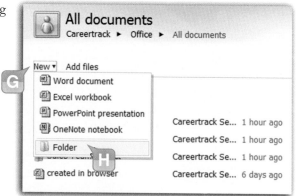, select **Folder** . If you wish to create a sub-folder, browse to another folder first, *then* click **New**.

6. On the **Create a folder** dialog page, replace New Folder with your title in the **Name:** text box .

7. Click **Next** .

8. Your folder will be created and you will be taken to the file view for your new folder with a prompt to add content .

9. Click the **SkyDrive** option in the **Windows Live** dropdown located in the top left corner of your browser window to view your new SkyDrive folder. Create more folders or sub-folders if you wish.

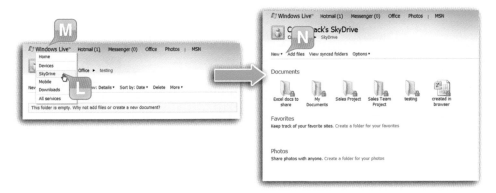

10. To save workbooks into your new folder(s), return to Excel 2010, open the file you wish to put into your new folder, then return to the **Save to Web** sub-tab under **Save & Send** in the **File** menu. To see your new folder(s) in the **Save to Windows Live SkyDrive** panel, click the **Refresh** button.

11. Click **Save As** button.

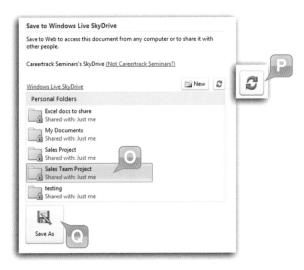

61 | Share Your Workbook Using Windows Live SkyDrive

Difficulty: ⚫⚫⚫⚪

PROBLEM You have a workbook that several people need to review and edit. You usually send the data to your colleagues through e-mail, but then you spend hours updating the changes into your original spreadsheet. Sometimes it's hard to tell what changes were made recently. You would like an easier way to collaborate.

SOLUTION Share the workbook on Windows Live. With a Windows Live account, your SkyDrive acts as an external file folder that you can invite others to access. All changes are made directly into the original workbook and everyone working on the data can see changes as they are being made. *Note: You must have internet access and a Windows Live account to complete this tip.*

Step-by-Step

Share Your Workbook

1. Go to the **File** tab, then click on the **Save & Send** tab  in the Backstage view.

2. Click **Save to Web** sub-tab **B** in the **Save & Send** pane.

3. Click on the **Windows Live SkyDrive** link **C** in the **Save to Windows Live SkyDrive** pane. This will launch your default Web browser and open a window to your Windows Live folders.

4. Browse to, then hover over, the name of the top-level folder that contains the files you wish to share. A popup menu will appear.

5. Click on the **Share** link, then select **Edit Permissions** from the dropdown .

6. In the **Edit Permissions** window, choose the level of sharing you want by sliding the selection arrow  to the setting you want.

- **Me:** The folder is private. Only you, and people you add individually via e-mail address, can view and edit the contents.

- **Some friends:** You define a limited set of people who can access the files. These can consist of people chosen from your Windows Live social network ("friends"), or from your contacts list.

- **Friends:** All of your Windows Live social network "friends" will have access to the folder.

- **My friends and their friends:** All of your Windows Live social network "friends" *and* their friends will have access to the files.

- **Everyone (public):** Everyone can see the files.

Share Your Workbook Using Windows Live SkyDrive   193

7. Define the control level settings for each level of sharing by choosing one of the options from the dropdown menus .

- **Can view files:** People with access to the files will be able to read and download the files, but they can not change the files or upload new ones to the folder. This is the default choice. This is the only choice available for the **My friends and their friends** and **Everyone (public)** setting .

- **Can add, edit details, and delete files:** People with access to the files will be allowed to make changes to the files, upload new files, and delete files .

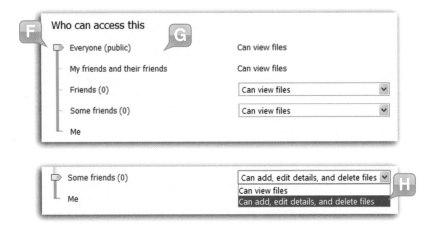

8. To add individuals to your list of people with access to your folder, type their email address into the **Enter a name or an email address:** text box .

9. Hit ENTER on your keyboard. Their name will appear under the text box with a control level settings dropdown . Choose control level setting for each person you add.

10. Click **Save** .

11. If you wish those who now have access to receive a notification, click **Send** in the **Send Notification for {Folder Name}** page. Click **Skip this** if you do not want to send a notification.

12. Your permissions will be updated and your approved colleagues will be able to access and edit your files. In Excel, hit the **Refresh** button in the **Save to Windows Live SkyDrive** pane. You will see the folder moved to the **Shared** Folders heading and the **Shared with:** notification reflect your new settings .

62 Invite Collaborators to View Your Shared Folders

Difficulty: ⬤◯◯◯

PROBLEM You have created several documents and saved them to shared folders on your Windows Live SkyDrive. You want to send instructions to your Sales Team, who will be reviewing and editing your workbooks. You need a way to tell them where to access the folders.

SOLUTION Send a notification with a link to the shared folders.

> 💬 **What Microsoft Calls It:** Send a link

📶 Step-by-Step

1. Log in to your Windows Live account by following the first three steps in the *Share Your Workbook Using Windows Live SkyDrive* tip.

2. Hover over the name of the top-level folder that you have shared. A popup menu will appear 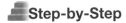.

3. Click the **Share** dropdown menu, then click on **Send a link** .

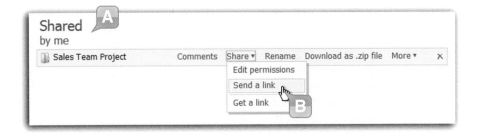

4. The **To:** text box will be pre-filled with individuals to whom you have already given access. You may remove people from the notification list by clicking the "x" beside their address 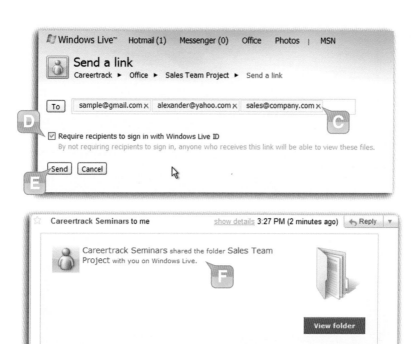 (this will not remove that person from the permissions). You may also add new people to the notification.

5. Click the **Require recipients to sign in with Windows Live ID** checkbox. ⚠

6. Click **Send**. An e-mail will be sent to each recipient in the **To:** list with a link to your shared folder.

Caution: If you do not click the **Require recipients to sign in with Windows Live ID** checkbox, anyone in your To: list will be able to view the files from the e-mail link, even if they are not on your original list of those you gave permission to "can view files."

Hot Tip: If you want to combine a link to your shared folder with personalized instructions, use the **Get a link** menu option from the **Share** dropdown G. On the **Get a link** page, select the URL from the **Copy this link to share:** text box H, then right-click to Copy (or use Ctrl-C). Paste the URL into an e-mail message of your own making with your instructions.

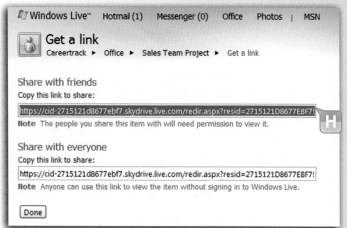

Quickest Click: You can **Send a Link** 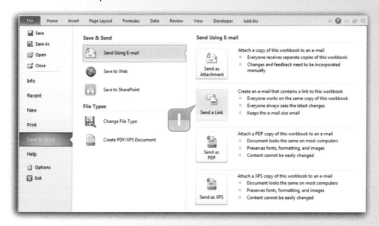 directly from Excel 2010. Go to the **Send Using E-mail** sub-tab under the **Save & Send** tab in the **File** menu. This will launch an email message with the name of the file included in the subject line and a link to the document in the body of the text . Fill in the addressees and your message, then click **Send**. Your recipients will need a Windows Live ID to access the workbook.

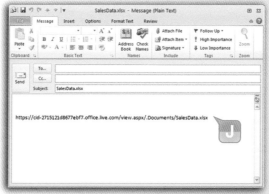

63 Customize the Quick Access Toolbar

Difficulty: ⬤◯◯◯

PROBLEM There are several commands and series of menu options that you use frequently. You would like a one-click shortcut to these frequently used tasks.

SOLUTION Customize the Quick Access Toolbar to contain the commands that you use the most for the most efficient working environment.

The **Quick Access Toolbar** A sits in the upper left corner of the screen, just above the **File** tab B. Any number of commands may be added to it C, and all items in the bar are accessible via a single click.

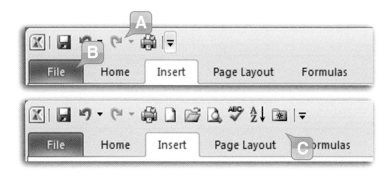

Step-by-Step

Customize the Quick Access Toolbar

Use this option if you want a broad selection of items added to your **Quick Access Toolbar**.

1. Click the **Customize Access Toolbar** dropdown button D.

2. Select **More Commands** E.

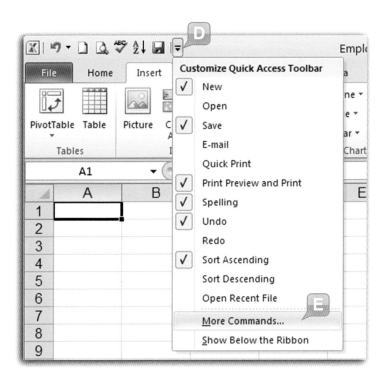

3. The **Excel Options** window opens to the **Customize** section, giving you access to the **Customize the Quick Access Toolbar** options. Here you can:

    - **Select Commands:** Select a command type from the **Choose commands from** dropdown **F**, click the desired command to select it, and then click the **Add>>** button **G**.

    - **Remove Items:** Select items in the right-hand panel and click the **Remove** button **H**.

    - **Apply your toolbar additions/subtractions:** Make a selection for only the active worksheet or for all worksheets with the **Customize Quick Access Toolbar** dropdown **I**.

    - **Adjust the order:** Select an item and then using the **Up** and **Down** buttons **J** . Moving an item up in the list moves it left on the bar, while moving an item down on the list moves it right on the bar.

    - **Reset the toolbar:** Click the **Reset** button **K**.

4. When you complete your adjustments, click the **OK** button **L**. 🔥

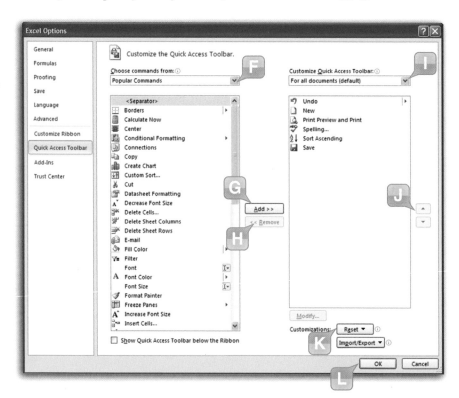

Hot Tip: Adding items in this way adds them to the **Quick Access Toolbars** for *all* Microsoft Office 2010 programs. In other words, adding **New** through this dropdown in Excel will make the **New** option appear when you are working in Word and PowerPoint, as well.

Bright Idea: Minimize the Ribbon. If the Ribbon takes up too much space, or you don't want to see it all the time, right-click the right tab and select **Minimize the Ribbon.** Click any tab to reveal its contents or bring the ribbon back by right-clicking again and selecting **Maximize the Ribbon.**

Quickest Click: There are a few simple items (such as **New**, **Print Preview**, and **Sort Ascending/Descending**) available as defaults in the **Customize Access Toolbar** dropdown menu ⓜ. To add or remove one of these, click the **Quick Access Toolbar** dropdown button ⓝ and then make your selection.

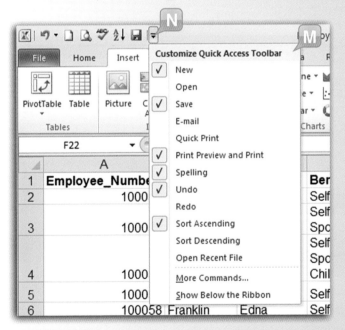

64 | Customize the Ribbon

Difficulty: ⬤◯◯◯

PROBLEM You have a set of commands that you use regularly. Several of these commands are unique to your work and are buried under several clicks by default. You want a way to bring these commands within easy reach.

SOLUTION Customize the Ribbon. Excel 2010 introduced the ability to customize ribbon commands to a much greater degree. In 2010, you can create custom tabs and groups, rename and change the order of default tabs and groups, and hide both custom and default tabs.

To access the Customize options, click on the **File** tab, then click the **Excel Options** button. This will launch the **Excel Options** dialog box **A**. Click on the **Customize Ribbon** tab **B**.

Step-by-Step

Customize Tabs

1. To add a new tab to the **Ribbon**, click the **New Tab** button **C** under the **Customize the Ribbon:** window. A new tab with the name **New Tab (Custom)** will appear in the list.

2. Right-click on the new tab and select the **Rename** menu option 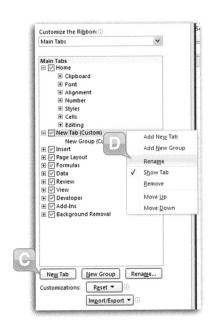. Type your custom tab name in the **Rename** dialog box 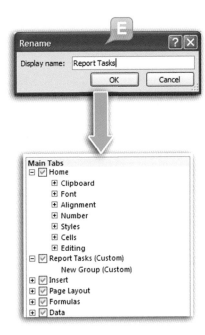.

3. Click the **OK** button.

4. To move your new tab up and down on the list (or right and left on the Ribbon), select it, then click the up/down arrows to the right of the window 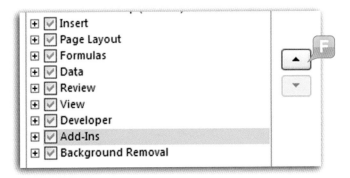.

5. To hide any tab from being displayed on the ribbon, click the checkbox to the left of each tab 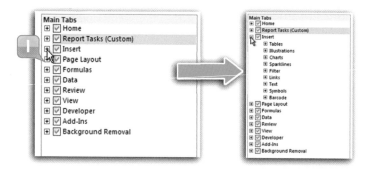 to uncheck it. Click again to unhide the tab and have it displayed in the **Ribbon**.

6. If you decide to remove a custom tab, right-click the tab in the **Customize the Ribbon:** list, then select **Remove** . *Note: You can hide, but you can not remove default tabs.*

Step-by-Step

Customize Groups

1. Click the **Expand** button to the left of any tab to view the groups that appear on the tab.

2. To add a new group to any tab, select the tab you want the group to appear on, then click the **New Group** button under the **Customize the Ribbon:** window. A new group with the name **New Group (Custom)** will appear in the list.

3. Right-click on the new group and select the **Rename** menu option .Type your custom group name in the **Rename** dialog box . You can also select an icon to represent your custom group by clicking on any image in the **Symbol:** selection box .

4. Click the **OK** button.

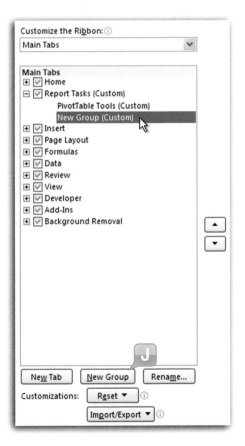

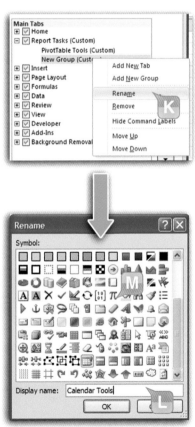

5. To move your new group up and down on the list (or right and left on the tab), select it, then click the up/down arrows to the right of the window .

6. If you decide to remove any group from a tab, right-click the group in the **Customize the Ribbon:** list, then select **Remove** OR select the group, then click the **Remove** button  between the **Choose and Customize** windows.

Step-by-Step

Add Commands to a Custom Group

1. Commands can only be added to custom groups, so begin by following the steps in the **Customize Groups** section to create a group for your commands.

2. Click on the command you want to add  in the **Choose commands from:** window.

3. Click on the destination custom group [P].

4. Click the **Add** button [Q].

5. The command will appear under your custom group in the **Customize the Ribbon:** list.

6. To rename a command that you have added to a custom group, right-click on the command and select the **Rename** menu option . Type your command name in the **Rename** dialog box . You can also select an icon to represent your custom group by clicking on any image in the **Symbol:** selection box .

7. To move a command up and down on the list, select it, then click the up/down arrows to the right of the window .

8. If you decide to remove a command from your custom group, right-click the group in the **Customize the Ribbon:** list, then select **Remove** OR select the group, then click the **Remove** button between the **Choose and Customize** windows. NOTE: You can not remove commands from default groups, although you can remove entire groups from tabs.

Quickest Click: Right-click any item in the **Customize the Ribbon:** window for shortcuts to add new tabs or groups, show or hide tabs, and move tabs up or down.

65

Choose What Is Transferred When You Cut/Copy and Paste

Difficulty: ⬤◯◯◯

PROBLEM You need to copy some data from one worksheet and paste it into another sheet with a different format to accommodate a client's preferred method of reporting, but each time you paste, the new format is overwritten.

SOLUTION Use **Paste Special**. There are times when you want to copy or cut and paste only some of the contents of a cell. Paste Special's capabilities are not limited to formatting and cell values. The **Paste Special** dialog box allows you to transport formulas, comments, and links to external data sources; skip blank cells in pasted ranges; and control column width.

See Also Appendix D for a list of keyboard shortcuts to access Paste Special

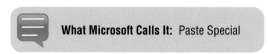

What Microsoft Calls It: Paste Special

Paste Special command can paste cell values, skipping blanks and using the destination cell formatting.

1. Select the data you want to copy **A**.

2. Copy the content.

3. Select the destination area **B**.

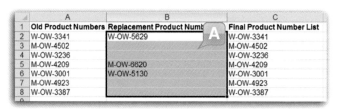

4. Right-click the destination area and select **Paste Special**.

5. In the **Paste Special** dialog box, click the **Values** radio button  (to insure that only the cell values, not the cell formats, are pasted). If you have blanks, consider clicking the **Skip blanks** checkbox (it will ignore the blank cells in the copied area and not replace those product numbers with blank fields).

6. Click the **OK** button.

7. Review the destination selection to be sure the data is what you intended to paste.

 Quickest Click: Several of the most common paste options are available from the right-click menu under the **Paste Options:** heading. Hover over **Paste Special** for even more at-a-click options:

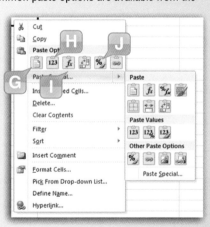

- **Paste:** Paste all cell contents and formatting.
- **Values**: Paste only the values as displayed in the cells.
- **Formulas:** Paste only the formulas as entered in the formula bar.
- **Formatting:** Paste only cell formatting.
- **Keep Source Column Widths:** Paste the width of source column to another column or range of columns.

 STOP

66 | Save a Workbook as a Template

Difficulty: ⬤〇〇〇

PROBLEM You create the same worksheets over and over for your monthly, weekly, and daily departmental reports. Each time you start a new one, you have to format the sheets and apply the themes needed.

SOLUTION Create a template. Saving a document as a template means that each time you open it, you are actually creating a new copy that you can fill in or customize.

There are three separate template formats available in Excel 2010.

- **.XLTX:** This is a standard 2010 Excel template.
- **.XLTM:** This is a macro-enabled 2010 Excel template. If the workbook you are saving as a template contains macros, you will want to save it in this format.
- **.XLT:** This is the 97-2003 template format. 💡

Step-by-Step

Save a Workbook as a Template

1. Open the workbook you want to save as a template. Make sure you have deleted all of the information you do not want saved in your template version.

2. Click the **File** tab A.

3. Click on **Save As** B. This will launch the **Save As** dialog box C.

4. Type a name for your new template in the **File name:** textbox 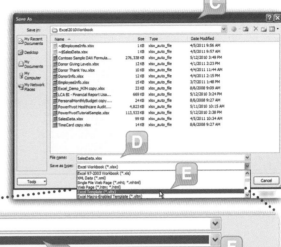.

5. Select **Excel Template** (or one of the other template formats) from the **Save as type:** dropdown.

6. Click the **Save** button.

 Bright Idea: Before you create your own template from scratch, check out the templates that come with 2010 or the ones available for download from Microsoft's website. To access these ready-made templates, click the **File** tab and then **New** in the left navigation pane of the **Backstage View**. Make your selection from the **Available Templates** section and browse for one you like. For downloadable content, click a category under **Office.com Templates** section and see if any of those will apply.

STOP

67 Create Your Own Fillable List of Items

Difficulty: ⬤◯◯◯

PROBLEM You have a set of offices and sales regions, products, and specific business time units (quarters, semi-annual) that you enter repeatedly. AutoFill would be helpful, but the default AutoFill lists do not contain these terms.

SOLUTION Create a customized AutoFill list.

C
Region 1 - Northeast
Region 2 - Southwest
Region 3 - Upper Midwest
Region 4 - Gulf Coast
Region 5 - Central Plains
Region 6 - Northwest
Region 7 - Alaska/Hawaii
Region 8 - Eastern Canada
Region 9 - Western Canada

D
Fall Semester
Midterm 1
Fall Finals
Spring Semester
Midterm 2
Spring Finals
Summer Term
Midterm 3
Summer Finals

E
Store 403 - Orlando
Store 709 - Kansas City
Store 992 - Chicago
Store 1123 - San Francisco
Store 77 - New York
Store 804 - Seattle
Store 634 - Omaha
Store 761 - Detroit
Store 1094 - Phoenix

 What Microsoft Calls It: Create custom AutoFill series

Step-by-Step

Create your own AutoFill Series

1. Select the cells which contain the data you want to comprise your custom list .

2. Click the **File** tab.

	A	B	C
1	**Store**	**Manager**	**Q1 Sales**
2	Store 403 - Orlando	Smith	$ 336,723.00
3	Store 709 - Kansas City	Jamie Wilson	$ 887,309.00
4	Store 992 - Chicago	Edward Cavanaugh	$ 228,476.00
5	Store 1123 - San Francisco	Bob Harper	$ 884,627.00
6	Store 77 - New York	Crystal Cogan	$ 205,737.00
7	Store 804 - Seattle	Jason Polito	$ 232,058.00
8	Store 634 - Omaha	Wendy Yaroch	$ 105,836.00
9	Store 761 - Detroit	Liza Bedgood	$ 847,265.00
10	Store 1094 - Phoenix	Steven Pence	$ 948,375.00

3. Click the **Excel Options** button to open the **Excel Options** dialog box.

4. Click the **Advanced** button 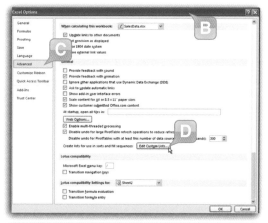 and scroll to the bottom of the **Advanced Options** window.

5. Click the **Edit Custom Lists** button to open the **Custom Lists** dialog box. This will also close the **Excel Options** window.

6. Click on the **Import** button to import your selection as a list.

7. Click the **OK** button.

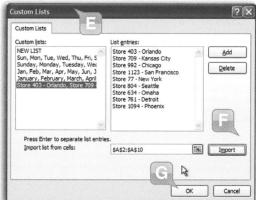

Bright Idea: To use your custom list, place your cursor in a cell, type the first item in the list, and then click and drag the **Fill Handle**.

68 Use AutoFill to Quickly Fill Cells from a List

Difficulty: ⬤◯◯◯

PROBLEM You need to enter the months of the year, for the next three years, into a column on a spreadsheet that will track monthly donations to your charitable organization. Typing the name and year of each month in every cell will take a very long time.

SOLUTION AutoFill to complete the series. AutoFill takes a partially completed series, three sequential months of the year for example, and easily extends it as long as you like. Even take a more complex format—like the month and the year—and extend it out for years to come.

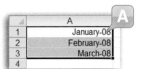

Step-by-Step

Extend a Series of Data with AutoFill

1. Type in at least three initial values for the series.

2. Select the cells containing the three initial values 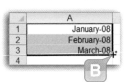.

3. Click on the **Fill Handle** when your cursor becomes a cross.

4. Drag to the desired number of cells and release.

	A
1	January-08
2	February-08
3	March-08
4	April-08
5	May-08
6	June-08
7	July-08
8	August-08
9	September-08
10	October-08
11	November-08
12	December-08
13	

Option: Click on the **AutoFill** button that appears at the end of your series and select one of the options:

   • **Copy Cells:** Changes all the cells to a copy of the initial values. January, February, March becomes a repeated series of January, February, March.

• **Fill Series:** Fills a series of data based on the pattern from the initial values. January, February, March becomes January, February, March, April, etc. Repeats at January.

• **Fill Formatting:** Applies the formatting from the initial values onto all the series cells.

• **Fill Without Formatting:** Changes the contents of the cells without changing the formatting of the destination cells. If the initial cells have yellow backgrounds, and the filled cells have blue backgrounds, the filled cells will contain the series data, but will retain their blue backgrounds.

• **Fill Days, Weekdays, and Months and Years:** These four options appear depending on what kind of information is in your initial data. Days of the week will only provide **Fill Days** and **Fill Weekdays** options, while complete dates (MM DD YYYY) will give all options. Selecting any item will fill in date information as described in by the Fill name, starting at the beginning date. A beginning data set of Monday, January 5; Tuesday, January 6; Wednesday, January 7; will yield only the days Monday through Friday, skipping Saturday and Sunday, with the correct dates.

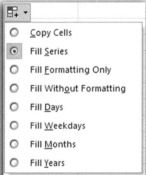

○ <u>C</u>opy Cells
◉ Fill <u>S</u>eries
○ Fill <u>F</u>ormatting Only
○ Fill With<u>o</u>ut Formatting
○ Fill <u>D</u>ays
○ Fill <u>W</u>eekdays
○ Fill <u>M</u>onths
○ Fill <u>Y</u>ears

STOP

APPENDICES

A Excel or Access: Which Do I Need?

What Is the Difference between Microsoft Excel and Microsoft Access?

In order to understand the difference between two types of databases, you first need to understand what a database really is. While we usually think of databases as being electronic, take a look at some paper-based information that could technically be considered a database:

- An address book of phone numbers
- A collection of documents
- A rolodex of business cards

An electronic database can take many forms as well. A list of information in a Word table, an Excel spreadsheet, and an Access file can all be considered databases. Some of the most common uses for databases include:

- Managing products, pricing, and inventory
- Tracking sales
- Keeping employee information
- Managing invoices, payments, or expenses

The two basic kinds of databases are flat and relational. In a flat database, all the information is contained in a single table, and each record contains a single reference and associated pieces of data. In other words, your left-most column contains an identifier, like a person's name, and each column in that person's row contains information about that person, such as address and telephone number. A paper phone book is a great example of a flat database. The listings appear in alphabetical order by the person's last name, which is the "reference." The pieces of information, such as first name, address, and phone number, would be in columns in the person's record.

A relational database takes the information a step further. It places information in multiple tables and then hooks them together when you need them. In a relational database, the information is stored in several related tables. This works best when you have certain information that is used over and over again.

Microsoft Access is software specifically designed to serve as a database. It has special features and functions that programs like Word or Excel do not have. Some of the differences include the fact that Access is a multi-user program, while only one person at a time can work on an Excel spreadsheet or Word document. This makes Access a great choice for company-wide information, such as product or sales data. Several users can enter data at once, and others can look data up at the same time. Probably the biggest reason to use Access over other software is that it is a relational database. The information is spread out into tables so that it only has to be entered and maintained in one place. This makes it easier to enter, easier to update, and less likely to have errors

When Would I Use Access Instead of Excel?

Let's say you run a food services company and you have a database that contains information about your supplies. Each product has a supplier and a category. These suppliers and categories are found on several different items. In a spreadsheet or other flat database, information is contained in a single line. The challenge, however, would come when that information needed to be updated. If you change the name of the Condiments category to Sauces, you would need to change it on every single item. However, in a relational database, similar information is grouped into its own table, then linked with the other tables. You can create one table to show categories, another table to show suppliers. Then link both of those tables to the Products table. When you change the name of the category in its own table, it is updated everywhere automatically—no more redundant data entry.

The same kind of linking can be done with the supplier's address. That address is used many different ways. It appears on many different requisitions and invoices. You could enter it each time on each requisition, or put that in one table and link it to the others.

Not only does it save data entry time, but it also reduces errors. If you had to type the address in 15 different places, there is a good chance there might be an error in at least one of them. Even a single error can make it difficult to search for information or pull reports later since the information is entered slightly differently for that entry.

A Excel or Access: Which Do I Need? (continued)

Key Feature	Microsoft Access 2010	Microsoft Excel 2010	
Storage Capacity	★	★	Both Microsoft Excel and Microsoft Access can store a great deal of data and a large number of records.
Security	★	★	Both Microsoft Excel and Microsoft Access provide a wide range of security measures across multiple levels.
Multiple Data Relationships	★	★	Microsoft Excel stores numbers and text. Microsoft Access can store formatted, or "rich" text, graphics, or even entire documentss.
Multiple Users	★	☆	Microsoft Excel provides basic sharing and collaboration on worksheets. Microsoft Access allows several users to access the same data simultaneously and includes information flow management options.
Consolidate Data from Multiple Sources	★	☆	Microsoft Excel can pull data from a web page or network location when you manually direct it to do so. Microsoft Access can be linked directly to external data sources for continuous and automatic data retrieval.
Create Visualizations of Data	☆	★	Microsoft Access can be used to generate reports and has simple conditional formatting options. Microsoft Excel allows you to produce charts and graphs, allows for robust conditional formatting, allows the use of SmartArt, and can export information directly to PowerPoint.

Key Feature	Microsoft Access 2010	Microsoft Excel 2010	Additional Notes
On-Demand Data Manipulation			Microsoft Access gives you some ability to manipulate data via table views and reports. Microsoft Excel allows you to review and tweak variables in tables, PivotTables, and PivotCharts and review the consequences of your changes in realtime.
Formulas, Functions, and Calculations			Microsoft Access allows you to program calculations and to run some formulas in particular sections your database. Microsoft Excel provides a wide range of analysis tools, calculations, and functions that work on all sections of your workbook.

 Performs well    Performs but with some limitations   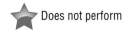 Does not perform

B Chart Terminology

Here are some terms you will need to keep in mind when working with charts.

Chart Axes: Charts generally have two axes—an X axis and a Y axis. The Y axis usually represents the categories of data in a chart, while the X axis usually represents the range of possible values that are being charted.

In this chart, a company has three offices—Beaumont, Regency, and Edwardsville. Each office needs to order supplies for their offce—wall calendars, employee handbooks, ledgers, and planners.

The **Y axis categories**—the items to be ordered—are in column A of the table and along the bottom of the chart. The reference points on the **X axis**, along the left border of the chart, are derived from the information in columns B, C, and D of the Table. Those X axis numbers give a guideline to help viewers of the chart read the data.

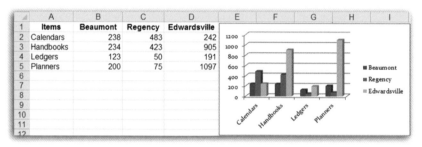

Values: Values are the data line-items tracked on the chart. In this case, each value from column B is represented by a colored pillar in the chart. The height of the pillar corresponds with the X axis reference points to show the relationship between the graphed items.

Legends: Legends are tables to help you read charts. By default, the legend on the right identifies how each piece of data is tracked (line, bar, etc.) and/or the color associated with it. In this example, the legend shows that the blue pillars on the chart represent the Beaumont office orders, the red represent the Regency office orders, and the green represent the Edwardsville office orders.

Which Chart for Which Data

Select the best chart type and format to present your data in the most meaningful way. If you need assistance in selecting the right chart for your needs, use the Chart Advisor. Chart Advisor is a wizard that scans your data and makes a chart selection for you. In order to use Chart Advisor, you will need to install the Chart Advisor from Microsoft's Office Labs site, but once it is installed you can access it from the Insert tab within the Office Labs panel. You can download Chart Advisor from:
http://www.officelabs.com/projects/chartadvisor/Pages/default.aspx

Chart Types

The following is a description of the major chart types available with some suggested uses.

Column: The column chart puts fixed data in a visual format. Categories appear horizontally and values appear vertically. Variations include the cylinder, cone, and pyramid chart subtypes.

	A	B	C	D
1	Items	Beaumont	Regency	Edwardsville
2	Calendars	238	483	242
3	Handbooks	234	423	905
4	Ledgers	123	50	191
5	Planners	200	75	1097

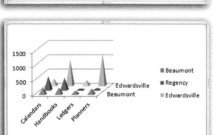

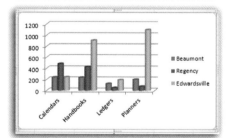

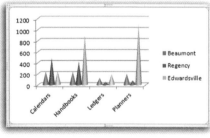

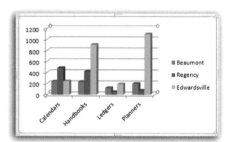

Line: A line chart shows the relationship of changes in data over a period of time. It is useful for identifying trends in data.

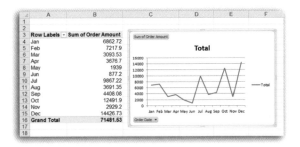

Pie: Pie charts contain just one data series. It shows the relationship of the parts to the whole. To emphasize the importance of one of the slices, select one of the exploded 2-D or 3-D pie charts.

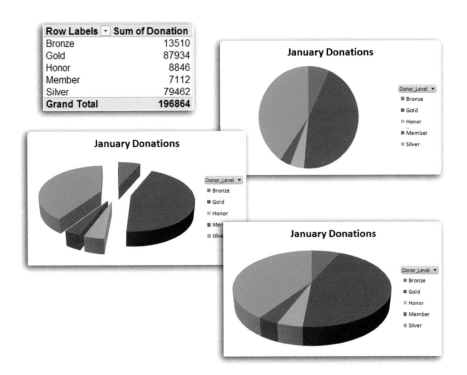

Bar: A horizontal bar chart compares items at a fixed period of time. This chart type also includes cylinder, cone, and pyramid subtypes.

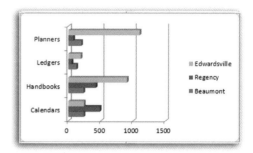

Area: An area chart shows the relative importance of values over time. Similar to a line chart, it emphasizes the magnitude of values more so than the line chart.

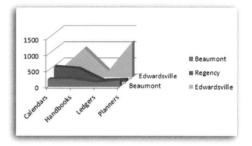

XY (Scatter): Scatter charts show a correlation among data points that might not be easy to see from raw data. It uses numeric values along both axes instead of values along the vertical axis and categories along the horizontal axis.

C | Formulas and Functions

The Language of Formulas and Functions

Excel makes it a simple task to perform mathematical operations. Using formulas, you can calculate and analyze data in your worksheet. Formulas are equations that combine values and cell references with operators to calculate a result. Functions are prebuilt formulas that can be quickly fed values without the need to write the underlying formula yourself. To use either, you need to know how to write in their own language, which is commonly referred to as operators. And, like any language, operators have their own form of grammar, referred to as Order of Precedence.

Operators Used in Formulas and Functions

Mathematical Operators

To perform basic mathematical operations such as addition, subtraction, or multiplication; to combine numbers; and to produce numeric results, use the following arithmetic operators.

Arithmetic operator		Meaning	Example
Plus Sign	+	Addition	=(B2+C2+D2)
Minus Sign	-	Subtraction	=(B2+C2-D2)

Arithmetic operator		Meaning	Example
Minus Sign	-	Negation	= −(B2+C2-D2)

E2	▾	f_x	=(B2+C2+D2)

	A	B	C	D	E
1	Items	Beaumont	Regency	Edwardsville	Total Needed
2	Calendars	238	483	242	963
3	Handbooks	234	423	905	
4	Ledgers	123	50	191	
5	Planners	200	75	1097	

Asterisk	*	Multiplication	=2*(B2+C2+D2)

E2	▾	f_x	=-(B2+C2+D2)

	A	B	C	D	E
1	Items	Beaumont	Regency	Edwardsville	Total Needed
2	Calendars	238	483	242	-963
3	Handbooks	234	423	905	
4	Ledgers	123	50	191	
5	Planners	200	75	1097	
6					

Forward Slash	/	Division	=(B2+C2-D2)/2

E2	▾	f_x	=2*(B2+C2+D2)

	A	B	C	D	E
1	Items	Beaumont	Regency	Edwardsville	Total Needed
2	Calendars	238	483	242	1926
3	Handbooks	234	423	905	
4	Ledgers	123	50	191	
5	Planners	200	75	1097	

Percent Sign	%	Percent	=20%(B2+C2-D2)

E2	▾	f_x	=(B2+C2+D2)/2

	A	B	C	D	E
1	Items	Beaumont	Regency	Edwardsville	Total Needed
2	Calendars	238	483	242	481.5
3	Handbooks	234	423	905	
4	Ledgers	123	50	191	
5	Planners	200	75	1097	

Caret	^	Exponentiation (squared^2, cubed^3, etc.)	=(B2+C2+D2)^2

E2	▾	f_x	=20%*(B2+C2+D2)

	A	B	C	D	E
1	Items	Beaumont	Regency	Edwardsville	Total Needed
2	Calendars	238	483	242	192.6
3	Handbooks	234	423	905	
4	Ledgers	123	50	191	
5	Planners	200	75	1097	
6					

Comparison Operators

You can compare two values with the following operators. When two values are compared by using these operators, the result is a logical value, either TRUE or FALSE.

	A	B	C	D	E	F
1	Comparison Operator	Symbol	Number 1	Number 2	Formula	Result
2	Equal to	=	8	8	c2=d2	TRUE
3			9	8	c3=d3	FALSE
4	Greater Than	>	9	8	c4>d4	TRUE
5			8	9	c5>d5	FALSE
6	Less Than	<	9	8	c6<d6	FALSE
7			8	9	c7<d7	TRUE
8	Greater Than or Equal To	>=	9	8	c8>=d8	TRUE
9			8	8	c9>=d9	TRUE
10			8	9	c10>=d10	FALSE
11	Less Than or Equal To	<=	8	9	c11<=d11	TRUE
12			8	8	c12<=d12	TRUE
13			9	8	c13<=d13	FALSE
14	Not Equal To	<>	8	8	c14<>d4	TRUE
15						

Text Concatenation Operator

Use the ampersand (&) to join, or concatenate, one or more text strings to produce a single piece of text.

E2			f_x =(B2+C2+D2)^2	
	A	B	C	D	E
1	Items	Beaumont	Regency	Edwardsville	Total Needed
2	Calendars	238	483	242	927369
3	Handbooks	234	423	905	
4	Ledgers	123	50	191	
5	Planners	200	75	1097	

Order of Precedence in which Excel Performs Operations

The order in which a calculation is performed affects the result, so it is important to understand how the order is determined and how you can change it to obtain desired results.

A formula in Excel always begins with an equal sign (=). The equal sign tells Excel that the succeeding characters are part of a formula or function. After the equal sign are the elements to be calculated (the operands), which are separated by calculation operators. Excel calculates from left to right, using the PEMDAS (Parentheses, Exponents, Multiplication, Division, Addition, Subtraction) order of operations.

In other words, it performs calculations in parentheses first, then it checks for multiplication and division, then finally it performs addition and subtraction. Using these rules of math can result in some potentially confusing problems that have many possible results if you do not follow the right order. Knowing that this is how Excel reads math, you need to structure your formulas accordingly.

$$2+3\text{x}4-5/6=?$$

If this problem were performed just from left to right, the answer would be "2.5." However, your intent might have been very different. Adding parentheses to show which items should be calculated first helps.

$$(2+(3\text{x}4)-5)/6$$

This same set of numbers with parentheses added calculate to a much different total. 3x4 is calculated first, for a total of 12. 2 is added to get 14, from which 5 is subtracted to get 9. Finally, 9 is divided by 6 for a total of 1.5.

D | Keyboard Shortcuts

Selection and Editing

Shift+F8 . . . . . . Adds other nonadjacent cells or ranges to the selection

Shift+F8 . . . . . . Adds to the selection (toggle)

Esc . . . . Cancels the editing

Ctrl+Del . . . . . . Deletes all characters from the cursor to the end of the line

Backspace . . . . . Deletes the character to the left of the cursor

Del . . . . Deletes the character to the right of the cursor

Shift+F10 . . . . . . Opens and displays a shortcut menu

Shift+F2 . . . . . . Edits a cell comment

F2 . . . . Edits the active cell

Ctrl+C . . . . Same as clicking the Edit Menu and selecting Copy

Ctrl+Insert . . . . . Same as clicking the Edit Menu and selecting Copy

Ctrl+X . . . . Same as clicking the Edit Menu and selecting Cut

Ctrl+D . . . . Same as clicking the Edit Menu and selecting Fill Down

Ctrl+R . . . . Same as clicking the Edit Menu and selecting Fill Right

Ctrl+F . . . . Same as clicking the Edit Menu and selecting Find

Ctrl+V . . . . Same as clicking the Edit Menu and selecting Paste

Shift+Insert . . . . . Same as clicking the Edit Menu and selecting Paste

Ctrl+H . . . . Same as clicking the Edit Menu and selecting Replace

Alt+Backspace . . . Same as clicking the Edit Menu and selecting Undo

Ctrl+Z . . . . Same as clicking the Edit Menu and selecting Undo

Ctrl+N . . . . Same as clicking the File Menu and selecting New

Ctrl+O . . . . Same as clicking the File Menu and selecting Open

Ctrl+P . . . . Same as clicking the File Menu and selecting Print

Ctrl+S . . . . Same as clicking the File Menu and selecting Save

Alt+' . . . . Same as clicking the Format Menu and selecting Style

Ctrl+K . . . . Same as clicking the Insert Menu and selecting Hyperlink

Alt+F4 . . . . Exits the program

Shift+arrow key . . Expands the selection in the direction indicated

Shift+Home . . . . Expands the selection to the beginning of the current row

F8. . . . . Extends the selection as navigation keys are used

Shift+F4 . . . . . . Repeats the last Find (Find Next)

Formatting

Ctrl+Shift+& . . . . Adds border to outline

Ctrl+Shift+!. . . . . Adds the comma format with two decimal places

Ctrl+Shift+$ . . . . Adds the currency format with two decimal places

Ctrl+Shift+# . . . . Adds the date format (day, month, year)

Ctrl+Shift+~ . . . . Adds the general number format

Ctrl+Shift+% . . . . Adds the percent format with no decimal places

Ctrl+Shift+@ . . . . Adds the time format (hour, minute, a.m./p.m.)

Ctrl+B. . . . . Sets or removes boldface

Ctrl+I . . . . Sets or removes italic

Ctrl+5. . . . . Sets or removes strikethrough

Ctrl+U . . . . Sets or removes underlining

Ctrl+Shift+_ . . . . Removes all borders

Navigation and Display

Ctrl+F4 . . . . Closes the window

Ctrl+6. . . . . Cycles through the ways to display objects

Ctrl+F3 . . . . Defines a name

Ctrl+Alt+F9 . . . . . Global calculation

Ctrl+0 (zero) . . . . Hides columns

Ctrl+9. . . . . Hides rows

Alt+F1 . . . . Inserts a chart sheet

Alt+Shift+ F1 . . . . Inserts a new worksheet

Shift+F11 . . . . . . Inserts a new worksheet

Ctrl+Shift+F3 . . . . Opens and displays the Creates Names dialog box

Shift+F5 . . . . . . Opens and displays the Find dialog box

Ctrl+1 . . . . Opens and displays the Format dialog box for the selected object

F5 . . . . Opens and displays the Go To dialog box

Alt+F8 . . . . Opens and displays the Macro dialog box

Shift+F1 . . . . . . Opens and displays the What's This cursor

Alt+F11 . . . . . . Opens and displays Visual Basic Editor

Ctrl+F12 . . . . . . Prompts Open command

Ctrl+Shift+F12 . . . Prompts Print command

Alt+F2 . . . . Prompts Save As command

F12 . . . . Prompts Save As command

Alt+Shift+F2 . . . . Prompts Save command

F7 . . . . Prompts Spelling command

F10 . . . . Makes the menu bar active

Ctrl+F10 . . . . . . Maximizes or restores the workbook window

Ctrl+F9 . . . . . . Minimizes the workbook

PgDn . . . . Moves down one screen

Alt+PgUp . . . . . . Moves one screen to the left

Alt+PgDn . . . . . . Moves one screen to the right

Shift+Tab . . . . . . Moves the cell pointer left to the preceding cell in the selection

Tab . . . . Moves the cell pointer right to the next cell

Ctrl+. (period) . . . Moves the cell pointer to the next corner of the current cell range

Shift+Enter . . . . . Moves the cell pointer up to the preceding cell in the selection

Arrow keys . . . . . Moves the cursor one character in the direction of the arrow

Ctrl+left arrow . . . Moves the cursor one word to the left

Ctrl+right arrow	Moves the cursor one word to the right
End	Moves the cursor to the end of the line
F1	Opens and displays Help or the Office Assistant
F2	Begins editing the active cell
F3	Pastes a name into a formula
F4	Repeats the last action
F6	Moves to the next pane
F8	Extends the selection as navigation keys are used
F9	Calculates all sheets in all open workbooks
F10	Makes the menu bar active
F11	Creates a chart
F12	Issues Save As command
Home	Moves to the beginning of the row
Ctrl+arrow key	Moves to the edge of a data block
Ctrl+Home	Moves to the first cell in the worksheet (A1)
Ctrl+End	Moves to the last active cell of the worksheet
End*	Moves to the lower-left cell displayed in the window
Ctrl+PgDn	Moves to the next sheet
Ctrl+F6	Moves to the next window
Ctrl+Tab	Moves to the next window
Shift+F6	Moves to the previous pane of a window that has been split
Ctrl+PgUp	Moves to the previous sheet
Ctrl+Shift+Tab	Moves to the previous window
Ctrl+Shift+F6	Moves to the previous workbook window
Home*	Moves to the upper-left cell displayed in the window
PgUp	Moves up one screen
Ctrl+F8	Resizes the window

Ctrl+F5 . . . . Restores the window size

Arrow keys . . . . . Scrolls left, right, up, or down one cell

Ctrl+Backspace . . Scrolls to display the active cell

Ctrl+A . . . . Selects all

Shift+Backspace . . Selects the active cell in a range selection

Ctrl+* . . . . Selects the block of data surrounding the active cell

Ctrl+Space . . . . . Selects the entire column(s) in the selected range

Shift+Space . . . . Selects the entire row(s) in the selected range

Ctrl+Shift+ Space . Selects the entire worksheet

Alt+Enter . . . . . . Starts a new line in the current cell

Ctrl+8 . . . . Toggles the display of outline symbols

Ctrl+7 . . . . Toggles the display of the standard toolbar

Ctrl+Shift+) . . . . . Unhides columns

Ctrl+Shift+(. . . . . Unhides rows

Formulas and Functions

Ctrl+: (colon) . . . . Enters the current date

Ctrl+Shift+: . . . . . Enters the current time

Alt+= . . . . Inserts the AutoSum formula

Shift+F3 . . . . . . Pastes a function into a formula

Ctrl+G . . . . Prompts for a range or range name to select

The "Magic" ALT Key

When you press the ALT key on your keyboard, letters appear on the ribbon. Clicking a letter launches the corresponding function. Unlike other keyboard shortcuts, ALT shortcut keys are pressed sequentially, not held down at once. This can be much faster than using the mouse. Here are some basic ALT shortcuts for you to use.

Alt+E+S+T . . . . . Opens the Paste Special dialog box with the **Formats** radio button selected

Alt+E+S+V . . . . . Opens the Paste Special dialog box with the **Values** radio button selected

Alt+E+S+F . . . . . Opens the Paste Special dialog box with the **Formulas** radio button selected

Alt+E+S+C . . . . . Opens the Paste Special dialog box with the **Comments** radio button selected

Alt+E+S+N . . . . . Opens the Paste Special dialog box with the **Validation** radio button selected

Alt+E+S+H . . . . . Opens the Paste Special dialog box with the **All using Source theme** radio button selected

Alt+E+S+X . . . . . Opens the Paste Special dialog box with the **All except borders** radio button selected

Alt+E+S+W . . . . . Opens the Paste Special dialog box with the **Column Widths** radio button selected

Alt+E+S+R . . . . . Opens the Paste Special dialog box with the **Formulas and number formats** radio button selected

Alt+E+S+U . . . . . Opens the Paste Special dialog box with the **Values and number formats** radio button selected

Alt+E+S+A . . . . . Opens the Paste Special dialog box with the **All** radio button selected

Alt+E+S+A+O . . . . Opens the Paste Special dialog box with the **All** and **None** radio buttons selected

Alt+E+S+A+D . . . . Opens the Paste Special dialog box with the **All** and **Add** radio buttons selected

Alt+E+S+A+S . . . . Opens the Paste Special dialog box with the **All** and **Subtract** radio buttons selected

Alt+E+S+A+M . . . . Opens the Paste Special dialog box with the **All** and **Multiply** radio buttons selected

Alt+E+S+A+I . . . . Opens the Paste Special dialog box with the **All** and **Divide** radio buttons selected

Alt+E+S+<*>+B . . . Opens the Paste Special dialog box with the **Skip Blanks** checkbox checked * Any letter selection

Alt+E+S+<*>+E . . . Opens the Paste Special dialog box with the **Transpose** checkbox checked * Any letter selection

Index

A

Action Bar   2
AutoFill   214, 216, 217
Average   42, 104

B

Backstage   4, 5, 7
Bookmark Cells   125

C

Calculate   48
Calculated Field   70
Calculated Item   iv, 74
Chart   v, 126, 127, 128, 129, 131, 134, 136, 224, 225, 226
Check for Errors *See also* Error Checking
Color Scales   82
Column Width   9, 11
Comma Button   33
Common Operators   45
Conditional Formatting   79, 82
Conditional Function   iv, 58, 59, 60
Convert Text to Numbers   28, 34
Copy   iv, v, 57, 210, 211, 217, 232
Copy Styles   27
Currency Combo Button   33
Customize Tabs   204
Custom Rules   84
Custom Style   23
Cut   v, 210, 211, 232

D

Data Bars   82
Data Filters   76
Data Tab   41, 77, 172
Date Format   34
Decimal Adjuster Buttons   33
Define a Constant   38
Define Name   125
Dependents. *See* Trace Precedents and Dependents
Design Tab   141
Developer Tab   118, 119, 121, 123

E

Edit in Formula Bar   63
Edit Permissions   193
Error Checking   62. *See also* Check for Errors
Excel Options   2, 215
Export Data   168
External Data Source   172

F

Fill Handle   46, 215, 216
Footers   148, 149
Format Cells   34
Format Menu   232
Format Painter   25
Format Tab   141
Formula   iv, ix, 43, 44, 55, 59, 60
Formula Autocomplete   52, 55, 60
Formula, copy   46
Formulas Tab   38, 125
Freeze   iv, 12
Freeze columns   14
Freeze Panes   15
Freeze rows   14
Function, Insert   54
Functions   iv, 56

H

Header   148
Headers and Footers   148, 149, 152
Help   7, 63
Hide/Unhide   12
Highlight Cell Rules   80
Home Tab   77, 122, 146

I

Icon Sets   82
Ignore Error   63
Insert Tab   97, 127, 135, 139, 146, 148, 169

L

Link Worksheets   164, 166, 205

M

Macro   118, 119, 120, 121, 122, 123, 234
Mail Merge   176, 177, 179